LIFE STILL ALTERED, TRULY: CONUNDRUMS OF THE LAW

Life Still Altered, Truly (LSAT I): The Legal Conundrums that Hold The Marginalized Back

By: Brennen B. Carter, M.Ed., MLS
University of Denver Sturm College of Law

"Studying marginality is as painful as it is useful: beware!"
-- Brennen Carter

This book is dedicated to my great aunt, Cynthia, who was a great community activist and the marginalized youth of America leading the 2nd Civil Rights Movement: KEEP FIGHTING ON.
Also, in memory of Demaryius Thomas, a wonderful Bronco and awesome spirit.

Written as a Socio-Legal MLS Thesis in
Social/Political & Corporate/Administrative Legal Studies

Published for Free on Blogger & In Print on Amazon (2021)

Cover Art By: Ruchicka Sharma, B.T.
Government Model Sr. Secondary School
"The Inequity in The Law" (2021)

Title Page Art By: Cam Cottrill, The New York Times
"How Rising Inequality Has Widened the Justice Gap" (2018)

A big thank you to the DU Sturm Westminster Library librarians, who were fundamental in shaping this work; the help is much appreciated.

"Lost in the crowd
And you can't feel no one, close to the end
Wondering is anybody there
(I'll be there, I'll be there)
The reasons are all gone
But the feeling still remains
And you don't understand
And don't you forget
When the sun isn't out
All you see is clouds
I'll be there
I'll be there
When you're feeling down
And there's no one around
I'll be there
I'll be there"
-- Rebecca Ferguson, Rogerseventytwo

Table of Contents

INTRODUCTION
1. "Introduction to LSAT I"
2. "The Most Powerful Thing I've Learned About the Law" – An Introductory Paper
3. "I've Felt & Still Feel" – An Intro Poem
4. "Theo-Foundations of a Legal System Entrenched in Socio-Contexts" – A 2nd Intro Paper
5. "The Bird with the Broken Wings" -- A 2nd Intro Poem

GENERAL
6. Intro to American Legal Systems – "The 'Law & Law Study' Problem"
7. Intermediate Legal Analysis – "The 'Law Analysis' Problem"
8. Corporations [Directed Research] – "The 'Business Law' Problem"
9. Law Practice – The Law Firm as a Business – The 'Funding' Problem"
10. Negotiation & Mediation – "The 'Bartering of Powers & Parties' Problem"
11. Leadership for Women in Law – "The 'Male-Driven-Field' Problem"

SOCIAL/POLITICAL
12. Legislative Drafting – "The 'Written Law' Problem"
13. Intermediate Legal Analysis – "The 'Argument' Problem"
14. Remedies [Directed Research] – "The 'Just and Proper' Problem"
15. Contracts [Directed Research] – "The 'Contract Specifies' Problem"
16. Negotiation & Mediation – "The 'Settlement' Problem"
17. Trusts & Estates – "The 'Planning' Problem"
18. Education Law – "The 'School' Problem"
19. Constitutional Law – "The 'Rights' Problem"

CORPORATE/ADMINISTRATIVE
20. Legislative Drafting – "The 'Legislature' Problem'"
21. Legal Profession – "The 'Client' Problem"
22. Corporations [Directed Research] – "The 'Corporate' Problem"
23. Administrative Law [Directed Research] – "The 'Bureaucracy' Problem"
24. Contracts [Directed Research] – "The 'Contractual Obligations' Problem"
25. Law Practice – The Law Firm as a Business – "The 'Law Firm' Problem"
26. Big Law – Practice of Large Firms – "The 'Big Law Firm' Problem"
27. Advanced Research for Legal Scholar – "The 'America' Problem

CONCLUSION
28. Conclusive Capstone Paper – "MLS Feelings – An Advocate of the Advocates"
29. A Law School Experiment – "No Accommodations is AKA Pain"
30. "Conclusion to LSAT I – The Pain of Studying Marginalization"
31. "Another Year of More Damages" – A Concluding Poem
32. "Still & Still" – A 2nd Concluding Poem
33. "A CALL TO LAWYERS – FIX THESE ISSUES" – A Final Paper
34. LSAT I Pt. II – Le Problemes Complexe

INTRODUCTION
1. "Introduction to LSAT I"
2. "The Most Powerful Thing I've Learned About the Law" – An Introductory Paper
3. "I've Felt & Still Feel" – An Intro Poem
4. "Theo-Foundations of a Legal System Entrenched in Socio-Contexts" – A 2nd Intro Paper
5. "The Bird with the Broken Wings" -- A 2nd Intro Poem

Introduction to LSAT I

"They say heartbreak always hurts the worst the first time,
You feel you're gonna die; you're blind, it's hard to see
Then in time you will find that you've moved on,
Then you'll risk it all to feel it all like the first time,
In a stranger's arms"
-- LEON

"Fuck arguin' or harvestin' the feelings;
Yo I'd rather be by my fuckin' self
Til' about 2AM and I call back and I hang up and I start to blame myself…
Somebody help!"
-- Kanye West

"Ooh, I can't wait to get home
I don't know why, but
I'm feelin' low
Happened again and I want you to know
Having my woman there is good for my soul
I try to be strong, well, I got demons
So can I lean on you? I need a
Strong heart and a soft touch
And you're the one when I want love
Ooh, you're there for me when I
Need you to be, 'cause I
Find it hard to say the words
But some shit don't need an explanation, baby
I tried to be strong, but I got demons
So can I lean on you? I need a
Strong heart and a soft touch
And you're the one when I want love
It's you and only you
That can be taken away
The shit that I go through
Each and everyday
Baby, I can't wait
In love with all your ways
Your arms are where
I wanna remain
Grab my waist when I start to say, yeah
Hey, baby, we can dance slowly
My, darlin', I'll be all you need, you need
I know it hasn't been your day or week, or week, or we-
So put it all on me
Oh my darling, put your worries on me
Can't judge me 'cause I feel the same thing
And I'm here for whenever you need, you need, you ne-
To put it all on me (babe)"
- Ed Sheeran & Ella Mai

    This book is an MLS thesis that I wrote as a law student at the University of Denver Sturm College of Law.

    This was my 2nd (or 3rd) graduate thesis (the first during a college-to-graduate-school-gap-year on sociological topics [*GWA I* (2019)] and another at the University of Washington College of Education in socio-education [*GRE I* (2020)]). This book will serve as a socio-legal thesis itself [LSAT I (2021)] (Sociology being a constant theme in my works).

The aim of this work was to present conundrums or "problems" of the law (in the US) that have made and continue to make it hard for marginalized folks in America. I also wanted to explore the ethics, history, end-results, etc. from the perspective of someone who sees the systems of law, education, business, society, etc. as (overall) well-intended and yet not as well-to-do as hoped. This stems from my life as a black, queer, and schizophrenic person and my lifelong pursuit of renaissance subjects such as education, people studies, business, the law, mental health, politics, and the like. This steadfast desire to study, read, write, and express myself has always made me a perfect candidate for law school as well as for social advocacy work on the behalf of others. It is part of my mantra to help others (while being well informed). As expressed elsewhere and to many: the quote on my ribs ("A life has no importance other than the impact it has on other lives") is a modified Jackie Robinson quote that has become my life motto that I truly aim to live by and up to. Also, I am prided at the fact that I have been around doing the things I do (tutoring, writing, advocating, expressing through art and literature, etc.) for something like a decade and yet I still feel like I've got a lot of "study mojo" left in me. I feel like a "savvy vet," not an "old vet" ▢. Perhaps one day I will indeed become as educated (and old) as I've hoped, and this 2ⁿᵈ Master's is shaping up to be the big go-before the other schooling I have debated in my mind (MBA, perhaps a Soc MA, a Theology Degree [late in life]). It's all a dream I'm running with, but so is being a very wise US Senator and perhaps US Judge, so the loftiness is just something I take with stride. I also choose wisely as to whom I tell my "villainous-like" plots of getting 4-5 degrees by 35, running an entire state, and being the same old me throughout. I pray that I am able to study through my MLS candidacy and thesis (as I did with my

M.Ed. course load and thesis) and study
through future coursework in a 3rd Master's program. Not to mention, I hope I can keep all that momentum and continue to write out these corresponding, yearly theses I have planned for each school (an LSAT book or two, a GMAT book, and perhaps finishing the GRE series I started with GRE I). If it were someone else that told me these plans, I would probably say they sound like an educated triple (or more) threat that'd be primed to be helpful to her or his fellow Americans in something like Congress or the court systems. I continue to pray I have the strength for the future I have planned.

Anyhow, the initial and
sustained purpose of *this* thesis was to aide advocates (lawyers, graduate students, activists, CEO's, influencers, and the like) in helping marginalized folks by acknowledging and naming the things about the law that hold these marginalized peoples and frankly us all back. This is not meant to outline fixes or even suggest changes, and this work is not a "guide to what we can do about the problems"; rather, this piece (LSAT I) is a starting (and talking) point to discussing how the marginalized face worse things than most (that's why they're marginalized—something is inherently pushing them to an edge). I am hoping, again, that advocates and the like can enlist this literature to "stay woke" about the problems with the law as it addresses the marginalized. Thus, you'll notice each chapter (or paper) enlists an issue (named "problem") in the law. This was a baseline I aimed for: "What is the problem?", not necessarily "How do we solve it?". Perhaps LSAT II will cover that latter mention. I really hope people recognize that focal point about this work.

This was a challenging and difficult piece to comprehend/feel let alone write; though, some fun was involved (start to finish at that!). I got the chance to venture to a brand-new city (Denver, CO), learn the culture, learn the law, be further on in my dreams (both scholarly and career-wise), branch out to studies that will be very beneficial to my career, develop a ton, and again, there was some fun involved. Luckily, this trial year of law school was totally worth it, especially considering my ability to write incredible works year after year at this point. I am proud to have worked through my past troubles and continue fighting "the good ole fight" no matter what city or state I am in. My year-long study (January 2021 – December 2021) would prove fruitful and meaningful, again from start to finish: this work being the fruit of acknowledgement for the sake of change—we are in 2021 by all (and after 2020: any)—means.

      I considered myself on two tracks in my legal program, though the U and you might consider those 2 perhaps 3 or 4 different subsects of the law. The MLS program at DU was super flexible / "Study what you, just make sure you're professionally developing through the specializations" so I was able to plan a pretty memorable, mixed plan for my year: I wanted to specialize in both social justice / socially driven courses and corporate law courses and thus planned my registration picks to reflect those two routes as well as slightly breaking into political and administrative law along the way.

      The courses (which have corresponding papers as outlined in the Table of Contents of this work) I took were as follows:

<u>Semester 1 – Spring 2021</u>
The Legal Profession
Legislative Drafting
Intermediate Legal Analysis
Intro to American Legal Systems

<u>Semester 2 – Summer 2021</u>

Directed Research:
(Corporations, Contracts, Remedies, Administrative Law)
Legal Practice Seminar – Law as A Business

<u>Semester 3 – Autumn 2021</u>
Trusts & Estates
Negotiation & Mediation
Big Law – Practice of Large Firms
Leadership for Women in Law
Advanced Legal Research
Education Law

The topics of the courses I was able to take (or research) allowed me the opportunity to surely seek out and attack the issues I set out to name as problematic and theorize about socio-legally. Not to mention, the style of law school was tough but good for me, so I was able to excel throughout the perils of law school.

So (here we go), the following is my first legal thesis: *Life Still Altered, Truly*.

> "Spending money... On things I know I don't need
> Cut my hair to change me... I'm smoking again
> Know how much you hate it... But you weren't here to tell me...
> I don't wanna know if you have moved on,
> And you don't wanna know if I have met somebody new,
> It's not as if I wanna run right back to you,
> I just want time to pass so I get over you!"
> -- LEON

"As the sun shines on all of my glory; My flaws don't look so bad at all
What was I so afraid of? Every part of me is a vision of a portrait;
Of Mona, of Mona Lisa
Every part of me is beautiful; And I finally see I'm a work of art... A masterpiece
Who is this I've tried so long fight? Filling my heads with lies that I'm not good enough
Then I heard something in my ear; Tell I'm perfect, now that I know the truth

Time to show and prove; Every part of me is a vision of a portrait
Of Mona, of Mona Lisa;
Every part of me is beautiful; And I finally see I'm a work of art
A masterpiece"
-- Jasmine Sullivan

"Just don't have too much fun without me; Don't have too much, don't have too much fun
Please don't forget about me; Try not to love no one
Oh-oh, try not to love no one
I know that that's too much to ask; I know I'm a selfish bitch
But I want you to know I've been working on it; I know it don't matter
I know it don't help you heal no fuckin' faster; Yeah, I know
I know I've been nothing short of a disaster
(Oh-oh-oh); And if it's too late (it's too late), I understand (I understand)
Sometimes it's too late to make amends (oh-oh, oh-oh-oh-oh)
Just hear me out before you let it go
There is one thing (one thing) I need (I need) for you to know
Just don't have too much fun without me; Don't have too much, don't have too much fun
Please don't forget about me; Try not to love no one
Ayy, try not to love no one, no one
Yeah"
-- Jasmine Sullivan

"The Most Powerful Thing I've Learned About The Law"

My dad was a corporate lawyer for Disney for 25 years until he recently retired.
I was pre-Law all 4 years of my disjointed college journey (and studied a mix of American Studies, Ethnicity, Drug Use, Business, and Sociology, while also going through mental illness).
I also have an M.Ed. from a top tier Education school and took PhD level (and some ungraded undergraduate) Sociology courses during the acquisition of that degree…

Still, I look back on all that time and I think, yeah, even today I consider this knowledgeable and simple statement more profound than anything I swear by in the law, and it is this:
"The law is made for the law-abiding and the law-breaking alike (and the law has a remedy for both parties)."
Basically, there is a reason to the madness and the law aims to be fair in its judgements and decisions; additionally, the law is prepared for all parties under the umbrella of justice and legalities. Simple: but intensely powerful, especially when considering the rectifying and fortified nature of "The Law".
Incredible really (and truly). There are no doubt issues, troubles (issues and troubles in the sociological understanding), atrocities, and problems in the law: but again, the law claims to always have a remedy for the rebel-rousers/criminals/con-people and the establishment/wealthy/well-to-do alike. The fight is theirs, though "The Law" takes both sides into account as fairly as it can (we assume in law studies). That is what has kept me

coming back to the law, more times than not (to be honest).

    The prior paragraph means so much to me when I consider getting this MLS, and it might travel throughout my studies as yet still the most important thing I've ever learned about the law: seriously.

> "You wasn't perfect, but you made life worth it;
> Stick around some real feelins might surface"
> -- Kanye West

"Who said I was an angel? What do you see when you look at me?"
-- Fifth Harmony "

"We used to be giants…. When did we stop?"
-- Dermot Kennedy

"I've Felt & Still Feel"

To feel,
Something so painful,
So real,

To feel,
Your heart,
It wanes as the pain grows
I felt for them, I now feel moreso
They said, "Your research sounds terrible"
I know, I know… But,
The more I learn the more I'm able to grow

Think about it a lot,
Cuz I'm in the same shoes,
But, hey, I'm makin it
And I even got something to prove
But little to lose,
So……..

I feel and still feel,
Something so painful,
So real,

Tell me, what do you feel?
You can tell me: for you, I'm here….
Year after year after year….

"I don't like,
Living under your spotlight
Maybe if you treat me right…
Then you won't have to worry!"
-- Jennifer Hudson

"Theo-Foundations of a Legal System Entrenched in Socio-Contexts"

TABLE OF CONTENTS

INTRODUCTION: "LAW IS A COMPLEX SYSTEM THAT AIDES OTHER SYSTEMS"

THEOLOGICAL FOUNDATIONS OF LAW

THE SOCIAL CONTEXT OF LAW

    THE SOCIOLOGY OF LAW

    LAW & SOCIETY AS A WHOLE

    CODING CAPITAL

    THE ASPECT OF COVERING

    THE PRACTICE OF JUSTICE

    THE PROBLEM WITH LAWYERS NOT BEING SUPER OR EVEN GOOD CITIZENS

THE INTERESTS OF JUSTICE & LEGAL ETHICS

CONCLUSION: "BEING AT PEACE IS KEY"

> "Don't let me drown!
> I know you won't"
> -- The Weeknd

INTRODUCTION: "LAW IS A COMPLEX SYSTEM THAT AIDES OTHER SYSTEMS"

The law is a highly complex and nuanced system of rules and regulations that regulates and in effect aides other systems such as business, education, any industry you can think of, and the like.[1]

The law is truly ubiquitous throughout the states: go anywhere in the US and the law will follow you ▢.

THEOLOGICAL FOUNDATIONS OF LAW

Law is considered history, precedence, rule, and regulation. It flexes the importance of justice in man and creates norms from situations (namely cases and statutes). Law, indeed, creates order and has roots in God and theology ("One Nation Under God").[2]

Past law is accepted as doctrine: often a sacred text. The law seems divine and boasts justice as its righteousness. Law students study to become "super citizens" and the law even mimics scripture and the like at times. It is centered in Christianity (for the good or bad) in America and embodies the system with which it regulates. It supports institutions, the rights of humans, (again) justice, and the state ▢.[3]

Justice and righteousness go hand in hand, and thus so do the law and theology.[4]

---

[1] Max Travers. Understanding Law and Society. Routledge (2010).
[2] Jacques Ellil. The Theological Foundation of Law. Seabury Publications (1969).
[3] id.
[4] id.

THE SOCIAL CONTEXT OF LAW

Despite its theological foundations (which are undeniable), the law is still rooted in society and its current ongoing (also undeniable).

To start: if law aides and regulates society and its functions, then sociology explains and studies society itself. We must not forget that the law is, indeed, people-centered, and the law is certainly cultured. [5]

The law has a) social conditions, b) social ideas/norms, c) people, and d) social constructs. The legal culture is a social culture and one that has theory, philosophy, sociology, morality, and nature in its functions. Many theories that explain sociological constructs can also explain legal ones.[6]

Law and sociology are undoubtedly tied together (by the cloth of society).

THE SOCIOLOGY OF LAW

Law and sociology actually are more than tied together: they have and continue to go hand-in-hand. Law and sociology grew together as major parts of the social sciences in the 18th century and on.[7]

Even today, many law students are culture buffs like me. The study of law is often the study of people, so it makes sense.

There is a merit to socially informed legal scholarship and the complex sociological analysis of the law as it works for people are the study of works such as this ☐.[8]

---

[5] Grana et. al. The Social Context of Law. 2 Prentice Hall (2002).
[6] id.
[7] Mathieu Deflem. Sociology of Law. Cambridge University Press (2008).

Law has many, many faucets, procedures, parts, and aspects that are sociologically driven (another undeniable fact of the law).[9]

LAW & SOCIETY AS A WHOLE

Law encompasses ALL of society in the US.[10]

It is a highly complex system that includes various traditions, perspectives, theories, interpretations, styles and differences.[11]

Law is also a global powerhouse. It is truly an incredibly diverse and vastly important aspect of society.[12]

Thus, at no point should the law be taken lightly in terms of the study of society.

CODING CAPITAL

Lawyers code capital by prescribing property rights.[13]

Freedom + Capital + Property Rights = The Basic Idea of America[14]

This equation is inferred from the book Coding Capital, which explains how lawyers basically make the world capitalistic because they regulate and somewhat

---

[8] id.
[9] id.
[10] Max Travers. Understanding Law and Society. Routledge (2010).
[11] id.
[12] id.
[13] Katharina Pistor. The Code of Capital. Princeton University Press (2019).
[14] id.

enforce the purchase, transfer, and overall being of capital, which is many, many things at this point (thus a need for many, many lawyers).[15]

It is also precisely this equation that makes lawyers uber-powerful and a massive force that could be used for good. The problem here is that many, many lawyers are not the super citizens we would hope for.

THE ASPECT OF COVERING

Covering concerns all of us. "Covering" is the process of hiding one's true self for the sake of saving face. Queer people do it, women do it, minorities do it, and it saves us but threatens our culture.[16]

Conforming to society's prescribed norms and sacrificing one's true self along the way is one of the most harmful things we can do as people and as a collective. Be true to yourself, speak your truths, and fight for justice.[17]

If we cover: we can't fight and aren't fighting for justice fully: point blank.

THE PRACTICE OF JUSTICE

Practicing justice, whether as a judge, lawyer, vigilante, or layperson, is an everyday thing. It's not just a case or a situation, it's a lifestyle. This is an important note in 2021: justice is an everyday practice.

---

[15] id.
[16] Kenji Yoshing. Covering. Random House (2006).
[17] id.

Justice means what is right, and that means trying to be in the right daily for all of us. Again, we can all practice justice and need to. It takes mindfulness to do so, and mindfulness requires health, creativity, problem solving, and critical thinking.[18]

Being conscious of the way you practice justice: barred lawyer or just guy at a bar.

THE PROBLEM WITH LAWYERS NOT BEING SUPER OR EVEN GOOD CITIZENS

The problem if the lawyers (super citizens with the powers of the law) don't use these powers for good are thus simply inferred from the prior four to six or so sections.

Bad and non-justice-seeking lawyers could (and have) open(ed) Pandora's Box.

THE INTERESTS OF JUSTICE & LEGAL ETHICS

Justice is concerned with what is right, looking to God and society for advice.

Legal ethics are concerned with what is right for all, as best we can.

Both can be bettered today.

CONCLUSION: "BEING AT PEACE IS KEY"

---

[18] Vinson et. al. *Mindful Lawyering.* Carolina Academic Press (2018).

During the holiday season of which I wrote the end of this text (Oct, Nov, Dec of 2021), my sister gave me a fascinating book that I read, and skimmed (I'll admit), and really enjoyed. The book is called *The Anatomy of Peace* and the key thing I took from it was to have my heart at peace. When our hearts are at war, we are invested in something that is damning, basically. Better to choose peace and calm for your heart, even if one is at war with something.[19]

That idea really resonated with me while finishing this thesis because I realize my heart has been at war for a long time, and it is time to let it rest and be at peace. I can fight battles with my mind and my body, best to leave my heart with warmth and peace.[20]

I know this is not easy to do, but I want to be at peace with my intentions and fight consciously. I can win battles without waging war in my heart. It simply can be done.

Let your heart rest, be at calm, and be at peace. Battles are best fought with a pure heart: better decisions are made.[21]

"I got a feelin'
You're comin' back,
Just like you have in the past...

---

[19] The Arbinger Institute. The Anatomy of Peace. 3 The Arbinger Institute (2015).
[20] id.
[21] id.

You're comin' back
Call me a telepath"
-- Conan Grey

"The Bird with the Broken Wings"

There once was a bird, a bird who flew so beautifully,

The way she flew, oh Lord, she was a sight to see,
The dips, the turns all the things...
You know they say, why wouldn't you fly
If you had such glorious wings?
But, much was put on the bird,
In the timeliness of things,
There was things that needed to be moved,
You know, for those with good wings,
But such a load to a bird could do so many a things,
And to this glorious bird, the things, well,
they broke her wings

--

Hard times
Hard times
Hard times, frustrating things
But as time wore,
This bird,
This bird,
This bird, who once flew so beautifully,
Well,
She healed and well,
That bird,
That bird
That bird

--

Now,
Well, it's certainly, again, such a sight to see,
Because this bird,
This bird
This bird, had.... well, to even mention the thing....

"My bad habits lead to late nights endin' alone
Conversations with a stranger,
I barely know,

Swearin' this will be the last
But it probably won't
I've got nothing left to lose or use or do,
My bad habits lead to you"
-- Ed Sheeran

<u>GENERAL</u>
    6. Intro to American Legal Systems – "The 'Law & Law Study' Problem"

7. Intermediate Legal Analysis – "The 'Law Analysis' Problem"
8. Corporations [Directed Research] – "The 'Business Law' Problem"
9. Law Practice – The Law Firm as a Business – The 'Funding' Problem"
10. Negotiation & Mediation – "The 'Bartering of Powers & Parties' Problem"
11. Leadership for Women in Law – "The 'Male-Driven-Field' Problem"

"The 'Law & Law Study' Problem"

TABLE OF CONTENTS

INTRODUCTION: THE PROBLEM OF THE LAW ITSELF

PROBLEMS WITH THE STUDY & PRACTICE OF LAW

    PROBLEMS WITH THE LAW BEING A DIFFICULT SUBJECT

    PROBLEMS WITH LAW STUDY BEING EXPENSIVE

    PROBLEMS WITH LAW STUDY & PRACTICE BEING BIASED

    PROBLEMS WITH LAW STUDY & PRACTICE BEING GATEKEPT

CONCLUSION: "INHERENT BIAS DESPITE ITS REMEDYING PROMISES"

"There's a she wolf in the closet,

Open up and set it free (Ah-oooh),

There's a she wolf in your closet,

Let it out so it can breathe"

-- Shakira

INTRODUCTION: THE PROBLEM OF THE LAW ITSELF

There are many issues/troubles/problems of the law itself. Plainly said: the law is a biased and often segregated system that relies on impartial people to decide the lives of common citizens. With tons of nuances and other troubles and trivialities, it is no wonder why one would need a lawyer to deal with just about any sort of legal issue (no matter its nature).[22]

This paper deals with the general issues of the law itself, including biases, difficulties, monetary barriers, and the like. This thesis as a whole will reveal many more intricacies that make it the law the problematic system that it is (oftentimes).

The law is literally a toughened, isolated, elitist, and well-paid profession that seeks to render judgements on any and all disputes that come across as legal issues.[23] This is empowering to the legal system and beholds them as the "regulators" (and not in the Nate Dogg sense) of culture, business, education, and any other field you can think of.[24]

Oh yeah, and *American law was created by white men for white men.* Black people were enslaved, Natives killed off, LatinX people moved away, Asians isolated, and all non-white people were demonized in the early state of America. Women also had no say when law was originally made to be the authority that it is.[25]

Today (as they have throughout American history): many of the same issues of bias persist (as seen later in this work and throughout this thesis).[26] So, there's a lot to consider about the law and law study right off the bat.

---

[22] Ideas from Professor Wald's "Legal Profession" course. DU (2021).
[23] Ideas from Professor Wald's "Legal Profession" course. DU (2021).
[24] Ideas from life as a lawyer's son and from being pre-Law in college (2021).
[25] Ideas from my American Studies & Ethnicity degree. USC (2018).

Finally, and perhaps definitively: *the law is the law, not always "the right thing"*. That idea must be made very, very clear.

PROBLEMS WITH THE STUDY & PRACTICE OF LAW

Make no doubt about it: studying law is tough. The study of law takes 3 years of rigorous study (if on the JD track) which is accentuated by multiple examinations, such as the Bar at the end of study, that are extremely tough.[27] Those without strong skills are often weeded out of even qualifying for law school and even if one can get into law school: doing well is extremely tough.[28] Many students will be faced with the unfortunate feeling of getting "C's" throughout schooling and graduating at the bottom part of their class.[29]

Studying the law is no joke, and the extensive rules for lawyers add to this even after graduation. All that is to say, oftentimes marginalized communities are often weeded out of law school due to cost, issues with past occurrences, the extent of legal language, and the general stress/time it takes to go through law school. This phenomenon is clearly evident by the numbers the ABA puts out about law school student and lawyer demographics (discussed in the subsequent subsections).[30]

---

[26] More ideas from Professor Wald's "Legal Profession" course. DU (2021).
[27] More ideas from life with a knowledge of the law (2021).
[28] Schwart & Manning. Expert Learning for Law Students. 3 (2018).
[29] Schwartz & Manning. id.
[30] This is in reference to numerous Model Reports put out by the ABA (some on law school diversity and some on law firm diversity throughout various years).

In terms of style: the Socratic method is preferred, yet difficult for many. As a writer for USNews outlines:

> For more than a century, U.S. law schools have typically taught students using the Socratic method, which involves professors interrogating students and demonstrating how to analyze court cases, and they have typically graded students through make-or-break final exams. But law schools are evolving to respond to changes in the legal marketplace, experts say.[31]

Though, this could be shifting toward more student-centered and multicultural learning.[32] This could be a major benefit to students with diverse backgrounds, but the Socratic method is still the mainstay in terms of law school teaching styles. In addition, experiential learning is also getting an induction into legal learning. As David Getches (a Colorado lawyer) outlines:

> Chances are that nearly every Colorado lawyer, experienced or novice-- regardless of having been educated in the East, in the West, or in between--had a remarkably similar legal education. We all took many of the same first-year courses--and second- and third-year courses, as well--based on case books comprising appellate court decisions. The courses likely were taught by bright professors who had excelled in their own

---

[31] Ilana Kowarski. Choose a Law School Based on Teaching Style. USNews (2016).
[32] Johanna Dennis. ENSURING A MULTICULTURAL EDUCATIONAL EXPERIENCE IN LEGAL EDUCATION: START WITH THE LEGAL WRITING CLASSROOM. Texas Wesleyan Law Review (2010).

law schools and who taught using the Socratic method.

The approach and the curricula have served us well. We learned to analyze and solve problems, and how to communicate under pressure. However, according to criticism from **law school** graduates, legal educators, and others, something was missing.

One of the most frequent criticisms about the current legal education system has been the lack of exposure to practical application of the doctrines and **problem**-solving techniques that are the stock-in-trade of American **law schools**. With an elevated consciousness of the importance of such "experiential learning," a major change in legal education is afoot.[33]

This shift is reflective of the need to make law learning more realistic and accessible for people that are not "traditional" students.

Problems with the study of law are expansive, and thus so are the problems of the practice of law. The following 3 sections outline a few of these problems in detail.

PROBLEMS WITH THE LAW BEING A DIFFICULT SUBJECT

Again, law school is no joke. In this subsection, I draw on the work of a University at Buffalo School of Law resource which discusses 5 differences between college and

---

[33] David H. Getches. What's New in Legal Education—Experiential Learning. Colorado Lawyer (2009).

law school and the Schwartz and Manning text (*Expert Learning for Law Students*) that describes what it means to be in law school.

As Wilson-Rew acknowledges, "Law school classes are taught differently than undergrad classes". This difference is evidenced by her description of undergrad learning as tending to focus on "memorization, short-term memory, and development of critical thinking skills." She says that "Courses tend to use didactic teaching methods (instructional or lecture-oriented)," and that, "the things you memorize may or may not be relevant to your major." She continues, by differentiating law school as more of an exercise in critical thinking, and "focuses on long-term memory recall and application of knowledge. Law courses tend to use the Socratic teaching method (self-teaching through discussion and Q&A)." These ideas are all consistent with the ideas expressed by Schwartz and Manning in their text, and it seems as though law school is driven, no matter the institution, by a lot of the same legal principles (critical thinking, case study, etc.).[34][35]

The authors give us more knowledge in the ideas that every bit of information learned could be relevant for the final, etc. and that law students are "expected to argue multiple positions and accept that a 'right' answer may not exist.[36][37] This is not easy for everyone to do, certainly.[38]

---

[34] Ashley Wilson-Rew. How Hard is Law School? 5 Differences Between Law School & Undergrad. University of Buffalo School of Law. (2018).
[35] Schwartz & Manning. Expert Learning for Law Students. 3 (2018).
[36] Ashley Wilson-Rew, How Hard is Law School? 5 Differences Between Law School & Undergrad. University of Buffalo School of Law. (2018).
[37] Schwartz & Manning. Expert Learning for Law Students. 3 (2018).
[38] Schwartz & Manning. id.

Law school studying gets worse. Studying in law school can often be incredibly demanding and hard for people and is a big reason for why many potential lawyers don't make it. It, "requires a different approach than studying in undergrad. The law is extensive, and you need a comprehensive, practical understanding of the materials." It takes more than memorization, which is hard for many students.[39] Law school study seems to be difficult no matter where you attend or how smart you are: there's simply a ton of work to be done in a critical way.[40] This may be good for the field, but is certainly a difficulty of the field.

Not to mention, it's also hard to get good grades in law school. Grades are often sparse (giving few chances to do well or make up a bad grade), on a curve (so grades are set in stone often), and are less personal (as professors often have less personal discretion in grading). In addition, law grades are often important for work purposes post-graduation, which is another hurdle for many students.[41][42]

There are yet other things that make law school hard to do well in, let alone finish and be bar-eligible (again, outlined by Wilson-Rew):

> It's more work just to show up in law school. Dress and hygiene expectations are higher. The atmosphere is highly competitive - law school is chock-full of intelligent, driven, strong-willed people. It takes more effort to stand out in that crowd.

---

[39] Ashley Wilson-Rew, How Hard is Law School? 5 Differences Between Law School & Undergrad. University of Buffalo School of Law. (2018).
[40] Schwartz & Manning. Expert Learning for Law Students. 3 (2018).
[41] Ashley Wilson-Rew, How Hard is Law School? 5 Differences Between Law School & Undergrad. University of Buffalo School of Law. (2018).
[42] Schwartz & Manning. Expert Learning for Law Students. 3 (2018).

She continues, stating anxiety and coffee are a large part of law school, and that many students commute and/or work. She says that makes for less free time and more stress of handling all the relevant business in one's life.[43] Law school takes a "reprioritizing" of life, time to recover built in, and a drive that is often unparalleled. [44][45]

PROBLEMS WITH LAW STUDY BEING EXPENSIVE

Law study is expensive from beginning through life basically (as student loans last 10+ years or more in most instances). Here is a basic list of costs throughout the law school process:

> **Preliminary Costs of Law Study**
>
>> **LSAT & LSAT Prep** – The LSAT can cost up to $250 without a waiver, plus registration fees, and preparation costs (anywhere from $50 -- $500+), which is a harsh entry barrier aside from the applications themselves.
>>
>> **Law School Applications** – Applications are also expensive, ranging from $60 -- $100 plus fees. Students typically spend $900 in application fees alone.[46]

---

[43] Ashley Wilson-Rew, How Hard is Law School? 5 Differences Between Law School & Undergrad. University of Buffalo School of Law. (2018).
[44] Ashley Wilson-Rew, id.
[45] Schwartz & Manning. Expert Learning for Law Students. 3 (2018).
[46] Florida Tech. The Cost of Applying to Law School and Why It's Worth It. Florida Tech (2015).

Costs During Law School

Tuition – "Over three years, a law student can expect to pay anywhere from $84,792 (in-state, public school) to $148,644 (private school) and up."[47] These are all caused by the following subfactors:

Discriminatory Pricing – "Top students often get huge scholarships, meaning the non-superstars end up paying more for their law degrees. Schools rarely give scholarships to people just because they're poor. As a result, students with the worst credentials end up taking on the biggest debt loads even if they come from low-income families."[48]

Faculty Salaries – Paying the faculty to make sure they can offer the product of a legal education is paramount to law schools.[49]

Parity & Rising Costs – Law schools often mimic one another in terms of pricing, and the general rise in cost of supplying education factor into the cost of law school.[50]

---

[47] College Ave. How Much Does Law School Cost? Average Law Degree Tuition & Costs. College Ave (2020).
[48] Erin Fuchs. 3 Reasons Why America's Law Schools Are Absurdly Expensive. Insider (2013).
[49] Eli Wald. DU Legal Profession Lecture. University of Denver Sturm College of Law (2021).
[50] Information from knowledge from Higher Education degree. UW

Return on Investment – Lawyers are expected to make a lot of money in their careers, so schools have little moral apprehension for charging so much for law school.[51]

Federal Funding – The funds are paid by the government, so schools don't have much issue charging a large price because the students are backed by the US Government.[52]

Set Cost of Attendance – Cost of Attendance is often set by certain factors that are often unchangeable or hard to change, so tuition stays high.[53]

Supplementary Expenses – Room and board, medical insurance, brews with the fellow law school students all cost a pretty penny.[54]

Other Expenses – Other expenses like childcare, gas, and other things that are often a case for non-traditional students certainly factor into the high cost of law school as well.[55]

Costs After Law School

(2020).
[51] Id.
[52] Id.
[53] Id.
[54] Information from knowledge as a grad student. UW & DU (2021).
[55] Id.

The MPRE – The MPRE ethics exam is around $125 on average. Prep can be in the form of a law school course or other prep materials that aren't too expensive relative to all the other costs noted in this list, but still one of many costs.[56]

The Bar – The bar is around $100 –$1300 depending on the state. Bar prep can be just as, if not more costly.[57]

Other Costs – Costs like taking time off to take these exams and the additional costs of "looking the part of a lawyer," etc. can add to Costs After.[58]

Other Exams, Applications, or Costs – Other fees post-graduation could apply easily. There are costs to being a "proper lawyer".[59]

PROBLEMS WITH LAW STUDY & PRACTICE BEING BIASED

Law schools are not as diverse (especially in some states) as we'd hope for. The graphic below shows minority numbers in law school by state, with many states falling behind the national average in terms of percentage of minorities:

---

[56] NCBE. MPRE Registration Information. NCBE (2021).
[57] JD Advising. How Much Does The Bar Exam Cost?. JD Advising (2021).
[58] Information from knowledge as the son of a lawyer. (2021).
[59] Id.

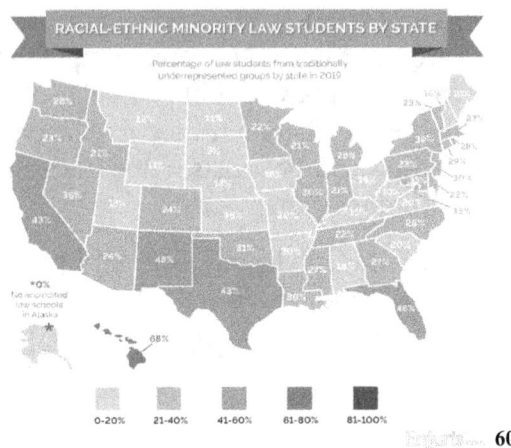

[60]

This is a problem that needs to be bettered. Minorities are 30%+ of the population and should be doing better numbers-wise in a plethora of states.

Other biases in law study/practice include: the Socratic Method favoring men's style of learning as opposed to women (given its "combative" type nature and it being very individual based)[61]; ethnic bias in standardized tests (the idea that white people often have an advantage in terms of the way standardized tests are written)[62]; white privilege biases and advantages (this should be obvious)[63]; law school admission and bar

---

[60] Enjuris. Law Sschool Enrollment by Race & Ethnicity. Enjuris (2019).
[61] Torrey Morrison. You Call That Education?. Wisconsin Women's Law Journal (2004).
[62] Roy Freedle. How and Why Standardized Tests Systemically Underestimate African-Americans' True Verbal Ability and What to Do About It. Saint John's Law Review (2006).
[63] Leslie Culver. White Doors, Black Footsteps. Journal of Gender, Race, and Justice (2017).

admission biases (whiteness bias among others)[64]; law school biases while in school (again, whiteness bias and the like)[65]; racial biases of law enforcement (police brutality issues, "color-driven" policing, etc.)[66]; racial and gender biases of courts and sentencing (the idea that white males have a better shot in terms of our judicial system and ideas of the like)[67]; political biases of the judiciary (another obvious case, though this one involving Democratic or conservative biases)[68]; crime reporting biases (think Karen's, etc. and other issues of policing, zoning, etc.)[69]; and jury biases (a trial by "peers" right?)[70].

Additionally, here are a bunch of figures as to how lawyers are not as diverse as we'd hope for (provided by the American Bar Association):

> Women are slightly over half of the population but are only 35% of attorneys.

---

[64] Paula Lustbader. Painting Beyond the Numbers. Capital University Law Review (2012).
[65] Penn & DeVries. D.C. Circuit: Study of Gender, Race, and Ethnic Bias. University of Richmond Law Review (1998). Nadler et. al. Familiarity and Sex Based Stereotypes on Instant Impressions of Male and Female Faculty. Social Psychology of Education (2013).
[66] Daniel Georges-Abeyie. Law Enforcement and Racial and Ethnic Bias. Florida State University Law Review (1992).
[67] David Gilman. Partial Justice – A Study of Bias in Sentencing. Crime & Delinquency (1975). Farrell et. al. Final Report of the Massachusetts Gender Bias Study. Northeastern University (2004).
[68] Eric Posner. Does Political Bias in the Judiciary Matter?. The University of Chicago Law Review (2008).
[69] Shea et. al. Bias-Crime Reporting. The American Behavioral Scientist (2007).
[70] Meissner & Kassin. "He's guilty!": Investigator Bias in Judgments of Truth and Deception. Law & Human Behavior (2016).

Blacks and Latinos are just over a third of the population but are only approximately 10% of attorneys.

In-house counsel senior leadership has shown a greater increase in diversity than law firms (which lag behind with essentially no increase at the senior leadership level).

The percentage of women general counsel of the Fortune 500 has increased continuously since 2014 to 25% in 2016.

The percentage of racially diverse (black, Latino, and Asian) general counsel of the Fortune 500 is approximately 10%.

The percentage of women in equity partnership ranks has increased less than a percentage point to 17.8% between 2014 and 2015.

The percentage of racial minorities in equity partnership ranks remained at 5.6% between 2014 to 2015.

The lack of diversity within law firms does not appear to be a pipeline issue:

Women constituting half of law school graduates.

People of color constituting a quarter of law school graduates.

> Women and people of color make up 45% and 22% of law firm associates, respectively.[71]

Women seem to be making some strides, but minorities and other marginalized groups are still needing to make many strides to make the lawyer percentages closer to those of overall minority and marginalized percentages in America (as to be more representative of the populations of people that often need the most help in their communities and lives). Bias is so pervasive in the field that some State Bars require training on implicit bias and the like; for example, the California Business and Professional Code requires:

> Training on implicit bias and the promotion of bias-reducing strategies to address how unintended biases regarding race, ethnicity, gender identity, sexual orientation, socioeconomic status, or other characteristics undermine confidence in the legal system.[72]

Even federally (in code, sentiment and otherwise), bias is recognized:

> In order to gain a better understanding of the nature and the extent of gender bias in the Federal courts, the circuit judicial councils are encouraged to conduct studies of the instances, if any, of gender bias in their respective circuits and to implement recommended reforms.[73]

---

[71] ABA. ABA Model Diversity Survey. ABA (2021).
[72] West's Annual California Business & Professional Code § 6070.5.
[73] United States Code § 12381.

PROBLEMS WITH LAW STUDY & PRACTICE BEING GATEKEPT

The law is gatekept (as in, that certain holders hold the power to determine who practices law) from top to bottom and start to finish.

The LSAC (Law School Admissions Council), ABA (American Bar Association), and various State Bars all regulate the practice of law and who gets into law study/practice. This entitles them with a ton of power. The law is a lucrative and tough system: holding power within it is massive, especially when that power is to regulate the (very powerful) practice of law. Not to suggest alternatives/solutions, rather the point is that there is plenty of regulation of the law at all levels.

In the research for this paper, a simple search of "law study bias" in WestLaw returned over 1,800 cases and 10,000 secondary sources that discuss bias in some capacity. This issue is massive, though when it comes to regulation of bias, there is not much to note of save the few statutes and rules that encourage anti-bias work. It is insane that there is vast material on biases of the law and yet it seems little is being done about it, which is truly sad and a definite problem of the law.

The leadership of firms, law schools, etc. also adds to this issue of law study/practice being gatekept:

> Firm leadership overwhelmingly consisted of white men relative to white women and racial, LGBTQ+ and disability minorities of any gender identity.
>
> Hires and promotions/attrition suggest that representation of minority groups is growing at the bottom levels of associates but is

declining at the higher levels of non-equity and equity partners.

Attrition rates were substantially larger for nonwhite attorneys (e.g., nearly three times larger for African American/Black and Hispanic/Latino attorneys) relative to white attorneys.

The percentage of white associates promoted to equity partner was slightly higher than the percentage of white associates promoted to non-equity partner. This pattern was reversed for female associates, and the associates of all other racial minority groups which displayed larger percentages promoted to non-equity partner than to equity partner.

Minority males and females consistently ranged between 0% to 2% of the top 10% highest-paid attorneys in law firms.

LGBTQ+, disability and the racial categories of Pacific Islander & Native American/Indigenous are largely missing from law firms or underreported in firm demographics, hiring, promotions, attrition and compensation. Most frequently, the average percentages were at or near zero for most of the analyses.

Firm size matters. Even within the same year, there were considerable fluctuations between firm sizes. Some of these fluctuations made sense as in larger average percentages were often reported among firms with 1 to 20 attorneys. Because of the relatively fewer numbers in these firms, any demographic group is likely to make up a higher proportion, often resulting in extreme percentages for a given firm. There were also some fluctuations between firm sizes within a given year that was not readily explainable.[74]

CONCLUSION: "INHERENT BIAS DESPITE ITS REMEDYING PROMISES"

The law is supposed to be fair, right? Maybe not. The law promises remedies too, but for whom? Who is the beneficiary of the legal system in America (is it white men?)? Who is the loser in this American game of law (is it the marginalized?)?

We, as citizens, nonlawyers, and lawyers alike must consider these questions when we study and try to understand the law.

This thesis evaluates questions of the like and is a needed work in the academic study of the law for the simple question of: "Who benefits from the law, and who is displaced by it?

"This is my age; this is my sign; this where I live; and what I like

---

[74] ABA. ABA Releases First Diversity Survey Report on Law Firm Equity and Inclusion. ABA (2021).

This where I'm from; and what I do; this what I love, how about you?"

-- Will Gittens

"The 'Law Analysis' Problem"

TABLE OF CONTENTS

INTRODUCTION

THE TOUGHNESS OF ANALYSIS PROBLEM

THE EXPERTISE & COMPETITION PROBLEM

THE ARGUMENT PROBLEM

CONCLUSION: "ARGUMENT PROBLEM IS HELPFUL BUT PROBLEMATIZED"

"Ayy, ayy, ayy

Ah, ah-ah, ah, ah, ah, ah-ah, ah, ah-ah

Can you turn it up a little bit?

> Ah, ah, ah
>
> Games we play, gonna stay up late
>
> It's too late, don't call me bae
>
> Nights turn days, my eyes gon' cross
>
> Get it real tuss, I'm feeling like a boss, yeah"
>
> -- Tinashe

INTRODUCTION

This paper is a brief analysis/argument about legal arguments and why they are often problematic. The conclusions are mostly based on my class experience in "Intermediate Legal Analysis," interactions with my lawyer dad, and a general knowledge of the law/legal studies.[75]

THE TOUGHNESS OF ANALYSIS PROBLEM

The law is complex and, at many turns, tough to take in and truly understand. If you've ever written a case brief, you might understand the complexities within the legal field that make it the protected/isolated field that it is (as only lawyers regulate law, not usually anyone else). Cases are tough to read; the rules of law are nuanced; and the legal practice itself is strenuous, challenging, and stressful. The law is a tough field to be in for many, and

---

[75] Few things were cited for this simple analytic breakdown paper.

many do not make it to be the lawyers they aspire to be / dream of being.

What makes legal arguments so intense to me is the framing of impartiality of law. Lawyers are supposed to be impartial agents who are generally not responsible for the actions/objectives of their clients. Think about that: lawyers are *supposed to be impartial agents* of the law *who are generally not responsible for the actions/objectives of their clients.*[76] It's kind of a wild proposition to consider, but a certainty of realization in law school and as a practicing lawyer or otherwise legal professional (even if not held to ABA rules).

So: argue your side (or consider both sides): you're not responsible or truly liable for the results, you just did your duty for the law….. I hope you're seeing how this is a bit off-kilter. Your client's objectives: you're not liable for. This is both helpful and problematic for lawyers and the legal system and is certainly something to consider about the law. Your client could have some pretty awful objectives for you as a lawyer, and it could be your obligation to put up a fight for it (think corporate clients, rich people, and the like).

All this must be considered when trying to understand the law.

THE EXPERTISE & COMPETITION PROBLEM

The law is vast and competitive: in many, many ways.

Law schools are competitive. I am at the 78th ranked law school in the country, and yet, we are learning a unique

---

[76] ABA. Model Rules of Professional Conduct. ABA (2021).

law-set (Colorado law) at one of the best schools in the state: school is still competitive.[77] It's less cutthroat than Harvard or Yale, but I was an honors student at USC, have an M.Ed. from a Top 20 Education school, and school is still hard/competitive for me. For real: law school is no joke. When they say you may need to study for 70 hours a week some weeks: they're not lying.[78]

Law firms are competitive. There is much to be said about this but is reserved for the papers about law (and big law) firms and other papers within the thesis (especially the Corporate section).

The law is competitive in general. There's usually a winner and a loser in the law (or at least some type of remedy and punishment). That's the pure nature of the law: it's how complex problems get resolved. This is the practice for lawyers and law professionals, which is often stark with competition.

THE ARGUMENT PROBLEM

The argument problem in the law is expansive, all-encompassing, real, and very helpful/problematic. Basically, the idea is that if you can make an argument based on the facts of the case and the rule of the law: it could help/hurt your client. In the study/practice of law, one has to consider all of the relevant facts of the case and how the rules are applied based on case law and statutes and the like. It's an intense process, because you have to think on both sides of the coin. This topic is explored in a deeper sense in the "The 'Argument' Problem" paper in this thesis.

---

[77] U.S. News. Law School Rankings: University of Denver. U.S. News (2021).
[78] Schwartz & Manning. Expert Learning for Law Students 3 (2018).

I give the brief example of my own law school experience. The course this paper is listed for (Intermediate Legal Analysis), we focused on animal and sports law, which was a doozy. It was interesting though, to write many, many documents on the "wild" cases presented and try and make arguments on both sides. The cases included issues like "pet birds" being "accidentally" let out of a house, "pet pigs" being chased to death, and skiers killing other skiers while going too fast down the slopes. It was intense. Though, the realization comes that the law is truly just arguments, which is an important note in any study of the law.[79]

Simply put: often, in law and law study: there are of course sides (and often the point is to win by beating the other side), and you've got to consider everything possible (both sides of the coin) to truly master the law.

Arguments are a hell of thing in the law.

CONCLUSION: "ARGUMENT PROBLEM IS HELPFUL BUT PROBLEMATIZED"

Any argument under the rules and facts is helpful because everything is considered but enter the Devil's Advocate in the second part of this work ("The 'Argument' Problem" paper). That's where the law gets heavier and heavier.

"He don't know my real name,

He believe that it's 'Sweet'"

-- Saweetie

---

[79] Diane Kraft. Intermediate Legal Analysis Course. DU (2021).

"The 'Business Law' Problem"

INTRODUCTION: "CORPORATIONS ARE PEOPLE?!?!"

THE DEFINITION OF CORPORATION & THE IDEA OF BUSINESS IN AMERICA

THE MAJOR PROBLEM OF BUSINESS LAW

ENTITLEMENT, ENDANGERMENT, ENCOURAGEMENT OF EVIL, & ESTRANGEMENT FROM EVERYBODY

CONCLUSION: "WELL... IT IS THE UNITED STATES"

"Boy, the way you blowin' up my phone
Won't make me leave no faster
Put my coat on faster
Leave my girls no faster
I shoulda left my phone at home
'Cause this is a disaster
Callin' like a collector
Sorry, I cannot answer"

-- Beyonce

INTRODUCTION: "CORPORATIONS ARE PEOPLE?!?!"

Corporations are entities that can be defined as people, as strange as that seems... Though, there is reason for it! As a writer from the Delaware Journal of Corporate Law states, there are:

> ... Three predominant conceptions of corporations: **(1) the corporation as an "artificial entity," (2) the corporation as a "bundle of contracts," and (3) the "personhood" conception of corporation**...There was a time when corporations were conceived as unreal, fictitious entities....[80]

In a nutshell:

> **This vision of corporations as "artificial beings" places the state at the center of their existence and activity. The state creates the corporation, confers power to it, and authorizes its activities. As an invented entity, it does not have a**

---

[80] Sagi Peari. An Assessment of the US Rules Which Determine the Relevant Law Applicable to Corporations. Delaware Journal of Corporate Law (2021).

"soul", does not feel emotions, and represents an artificial enterprise created by the state. **It is not surprising that corporations were seen as intimately attached to the will and existence of the state**, originating as they did within the historical context of large, public enterprises that performed such tasks as building public infrastructure. **They were viewed as holding only those rights that the state explicitly granted them.** This explains the other name given to the "fictitious" theory of corporation--the "concession" theory.

A second perspective on corporations emphasizes their governance and structure. With an emphasis on the inherently contractual aspects of these elements, this vision perceives corporations as a "bundle" or "nexus" of contracts ("nexus-contracts theory"). It focuses on a complex web of *492 contractual arrangements between the various corporate actors: shareholders, directors, officers and stakeholders. Presented in these terms, **the nexus-contracts theory of corporation does not challenge the "fiction" theory, but rather, complements it: while the latter evaluates corporate existence from an external point of view, the former provides an internal viewpoint that analyzes corporate content and structure.**

Today, the predominant view challenges these notions. Corporations are now viewed as independent moral actors; their conduct is unrelated to the states of their creation and to the complex web of agreements within the corporate structure. Originating in the writings of Otto von Gierke and Frederic Maitland, the idea of corporate personality insists that corporations have their own autonomous existence. This vision of corporations conceptually **separates corporations from the state that grants permission for incorporation (under the state-based fiction theory) and from the cluster of contracts that make up a corporation (under the nexus-contracts theory).** The normative status of corporations does not depend on states, nor on the contractual relationships that comprise it. Stated in these terms, **corporations claim their normative independence.**[81]

---

[81] id.

One article asks around the question of the fact that there has been stark debate as to companies' rights, namely to free speech (a couple links that contest on the debate are footnoted).[82]:

> **To what extent should corporations be given constitutional and statutory rights? Should businesses have social responsibilities toward the public at large? When should shareholders be personally liable for the debts of a corporation? How can legal entities become liable under tort and criminal laws?**[83]

(And does this section read like a "business law legal contract"? Yup! read the fine print!).

THE DEFINITION OF CORPORATION & THE IDEA OF BUSINESS IN AMERICA

Corporations might be more expansive than one might think. Nonprofits being corporations are a good example.

In addition, corporations accumulate business associations, business organizations, and different types of businesses in their ranks. Corporations, as defined in two different mindsets and one idea, are defined by *Corporations in a Nutshell* and myself as follows:

1. The Traditional View: As described by the book:

---

[82] Susanna Ripken. Corporate First Amendment Rights After Citizens United. University of Penn Law Journal (2011); & Lyman Johnson. Law and Legal Theory in the History of Corporate Responsibility. Seattle University Law Review (2012).

[83] Martin Petrin. Reconceptualizing the Theory of a Firm. Penn State Law Review (2013).

> **The traditional theoretical view is that a corporation is an *artificial person* [rather than a *natural person*]... the corporation is an entity, independent of the people who form it, own it, and run it... has many of the legal rights of a natural person** [sue and be sued, apply for licensing, hire, invest, buy and see, and must pay taxes].[84]

In this view, the people who run/start it are not responsible for its debts, the entity must act in accord with the people running it, though the corporations are subject to questions of "fairness, justice, or policy."[85]

2. The "Privilege" or "Contract View": Also described by the book:

> **Another metaphorical view is that the corporation is a privilege from the state, which permits the owners and investors to conduct business in the corporate form...** [the process of incorporating in America was once tough, but now] incorporating is so easy that the privilege theory still has some impact in the ongoing debate over the social role or corporations...

> **Another view is that the document forming the corporation—usually called the articles...--may be seen as a contract or a compact... The court may see the corporate articles as a contract among shareholders or between the shareholders and the state.**[86]

This view is separate but could be seen in the same light. Personally, I agree with both. I believe that corporations are both: their own entity (though "personhood" is a stretch) and a "privilege" for its affiliates.

---

[84] Richard Freer. Corporations in a Nutshell. 8 Nutshell Series. (2020)
[85] id.
[86] id.

3. The Idea of Business in America

I think the general idea of business in America is the idea that people, within proper regulation and capital, are able to form these "people-esque" entities that can contribute to the world as businesses whether they be buying, selling, offering a good and/or service, and the like.

I also think that lawyers enable these entities (especially the massive corporations) to do things not necessarily in the ability-range of "natural persons," which is a bit troublesome, though often understood when the same entity is important and/or employs a lot of people.

But can you not see the inherent issues with this enablement of greed, pride, using lawyers for evil, etc., etc.?

THE MAJOR PROBLEM OF BUSINESS LAW

Georgetown Law outlines corporate law, stating:

Corporate lawyers advise businesses (which can include different entities such as partnerships, publicly and privately held companies, and business start-ups, among others) on their numerous legal rights, responsibilities and obligations. General corporate practice involves handling a wide range of legal and business issues. Many corporate lawyers work in law firms, particularly large or mid-size firms, where they counsel clients and handle transactions including negotiation, drafting, and review of contracts and other agreements. Other corporate lawyers are employed directly by corporations as in-house corporate counsel. In-house counsel act as internal advisers on myriad business and legal issues, including labor and employment issues, intellectual property issues, contractual issues and liability issues. Clients are frequently for-profit, but non-profit corporations also rely on corporate counsel.

A corporate law practice may vary substantially in both the degree of emphasis and the type of practice. Some large law firms, for example, may expect their attorneys to focus on transactional work, while others combine transactional and litigation practices.[87]

A law firm (Merrill, Arnone, & Jones, LLP.) continues this discussion:

> **Business law deals with everything from the creation of new business to any issues that can arise while operating, such as tax law, intellectual property, real estate, sales, employment, bankruptcy, contracts, and more.**
>
> **As businesses and business owners interact with the public, other companies, or the government, legal assistance is always beneficial. Business law functions to establish legal standards, resolve disputes, and protect rights.**
>
> Features of business law include all the ways that an experienced attorney can protect your business such as intellectual property (IP) law for trademarks, copyrights, and patents to help protect your ideas and employment law that provides advice on handling employee rights and responsibilities.
>
> **Each business, large or small, is its own legal entity that must comply with government and state legal regulations.**[88]

And Harvard Law outlines:

> **There are five of these characteristics, most of which will be easily recognizable to anyone familiar with business affairs. They are: legal personality, limited liability, transferable shares, delegated management under a board structure, and investor ownership.** These characteristics respond—in ways we will explore—to the economic exigencies of the large modern business enterprise. Thus, corporate law everywhere must, of necessity, provide for them. To be sure, there are other forms of business enterprise that lack one or more of these characteristics. But the

---

[87] Georgetown Law. Corporate Law. Georgetown Law (2021).
[88] Merrill, Arnone, & Jones, LLP., What is Business Law? Merrill, Arnon & Jones, LLP (2021).

remarkable fact—and the fact that we wish to stress—is that, **in market economies, almost all large-scale business firms adopt a legal form that possesses all five of the basic characteristics of the business corporation. Indeed, most small jointly-owned firms adopt this corporate form as well, although sometimes with deviations from one or more of the five basic characteristics to fit their special needs.**[89]

Continuing on, Cronus Law outlines the various types (generally) of corporate law. These categories are broad but a good showing of the industry:

>Employment Law
>Immigration Law
>Consumer Goods Sales
>Contract Drafting/Negotiations/Litigation
>Antitrust
>Intellectual Property
>Taxes
>Bankruptcy
>Business Formation
>Contracts
>Lawsuits[90]

Forbes outlines 3 top reasons why corporate compliance (i.e., lawyers are necessary here) is important, stating:

1. It Improves Overall Operations
2. It Saves the Company Money
3. Makes the Company More Competitive[91]

Finally, Jacob Maslow, a Legal Scoops writer discusses the legal issues businesspeople face, which namely are:

---

[89] Armour et. al. The Essential Elements of Corporate Law. Harvard Law (2009).

[90] Cronus Law. What Is Business Law & The Different Types (With Examples). Cronus Law (2019).

[91] Thomas Sehested. Why Compliance Is A Business Enabler, Not A Hindrance. Forbes (2018).

1. Business formation
2. Licensing
3. Employee and partner agreements
4. Cases of discrimination and harassment
5. Misclassification of employees
6. Copyrights, patents, and trademarks
7. Lawsuits by dissatisfied customers[92]

What's left unstated in this discussion of corporate law is the fact that lawyers enable many companies to do the evil they do. This, of course, is discussed in the next section.

ENTITLEMENT, ENDANGERMENT, ENCOURAGEMENT OF EVIL, & ESTRANGEMENT FROM EVERYBODY

I could have utilized a ton of sources in this discussion section, but I think my own takes on "Business in America" should suffice:

1. **Entitlement:** Limited liability creates space in which people and entities feel free, creative, inspiring, and all the like. But it also creates a sense of entitlement only business in America (and perhaps in a couple other places around the globe) know. This idea that "money is king" or that "profits are over purpose" are a problem of business and thus one of business's enabler: business law.
2. **Endangerment:** Business law, by allowing corporations to operate as "profit at all costs" are dangerous and endanger a lot of people. Corporate dumping, overuse of plastic, environmental harm in general, can all be attributed to corporations and

---

[92] Jacob Maslow. 7 Most Common Legal Problems Businesses Face in Their Operations. Legal Scoops (2020).

their endangerment of the world. Here is a reference to Global Issues' article about corporations harming the environment.[93]

3. **Encouragement of Evil:** Profits over people: my main issue with businesses. This, and many other business practices by top companies in this country, are problematic as they often encourage evilness in people and in entities.
4. **Estrangement from Everybody:** Companies can often isolate people from people. If you don't think so: watch entitled "Karen" videos and the ways expert customer service agents handle them. It is a marvel to see, though the "Karen's" are caused by this estrangement of corporations, their workers, and people. Here are three lists of customer service horror stories.[94] Karen's usually a) misinterpret the policies of a business or government and b) overstep and overestimate their rights. Workers are often trained to be impartial (as to avoid discrimination) and the business is its own entity oftentimes, which leads to trouble for the workers as the business aims to remain impartial despite the nuttiness of Karen's. It's a cycle of entitlement and limited liability that leave customer service agents, waitresses, managers, etc. left to bear the brunt of ridiculousness from customers.[95]

---

[93] Global Issues. Corporations and the Environment. Global Issues (2002).
[94] Les Melnichenko. 9 Customer Service Horror Stories that Will Make Your Blood Turn to Ice. Help Crunch (2020).; Isha Bassi. 26 Unbelievable Customer Service Stories That Sound Like Literal Nightmares. Buzzfeed (2018).; Steven McDonald. 13 Gruesome (and Spine-Chilling) Customer Service Horror Stories (2020).

[95] Information from analyzing dozens upon dozens of "Karen gon Wild" videos.

There is certainly a problem with such. I have seen too many videos to say otherwise.

CONCLUSION: "WELL... IT IS THE UNITED STATES"

If America's businesses are indeed its heartbeat... what can we do but help it get better, rather than cancel or significantly alter its nature?

Corporations are necessary for America: like it or not, but the problem is: how do we improve them holistically?

Well... It is the United States....

"I've been sitting on the charts like a beach chair

My last album, spent 52 weeks there

Almost finished with the second, you should be scared

Storms coming you should go inside and prepare

No shortcuts, it ain't no cheats there

I brought the whole city out like a street fair

And fuck it I'm the coldest white rapper in the game

Since the one with the bleached hair

Yeah, they love it when I talk shit

I get around, yeah I'm on my 2Pac shit

I kinda feel there's no girl I could not get

I'm not found at the function if it's not lit

Yeah, it's Nathan that no one can tell me

I made it here dolo, nobody to help me

From the Bay, the birthplace of the hyphy

So bitch come and say to my face you don't like me"

-- G Eazy

"The 'Corporate' Problem"

INTRODUCTION: SO WHAT? I'M A CORPORATE & SOCIAL LAW STUDENT; GET OVER IT AND YOURSELF

ARGUMENTS WITH FRIENDS OVER "CORPORATIONS"

CORPORATIONS IN GENERAL

    GENERAL ARGUMENTS FOR CORPORATIONS

    GENERAL ARGUMENTS AGAINST CORPORATIONS

A "CONSERVATIVE SOCIALIST" IDEOLOGY

CONCLUSION: BUSINESS IS THE HEARTBEAT OF AMERICA, JUST TO BE HONEST, BUT...

Fast, I'm coming in fast (uh-huh); First place, you coming in last (that's right)

I'm hitting that, hitting that gas; I'm hitting that, hitting that ass (my body)

I'm coming in fast (uh-huh); First place, you coming in last

I'm hitting that, hitting that gas; I'm hitting that, hitting that

Locomotion; We causing a commotion

I put it in, I put it in, I put it in motion; I put it in, I put it in, I put it in motion

Locomotion; We causing a commotion

Iciest bitch in the whole damn land; I hit the road in an all-white Lam'

I keep a fresh set up on my hands; You don't like me, but you on my 'Gram

How you look, how you look, how you sound, ho?; I'm a boss, I'm a brat, hard to handle

I'm a real life mood, a real life muse; Got some pretty-ass toes in my sandals

I can't help, I was born like this; Ain't my fault that you want my drip

Little bitter bitch could have been my friend; Now you gotta listen while I pop my shit"

-- Saweetie

INTRODUCTION: SO WHAT? I'M A CORPORATE & SOCIAL LAW STUDENT; GET OVER IT AND YOURSELF

Most people, when I tell them (which is rare) that I study corporate law in addition to socially driven law, they are often a) put off, b) wondering why I study corporations, and c) decently snarky about their disdain for corporations. Corporations are a toss-up to me though, and I think many, many people have the same sentiment towards these entities. So, I take it with a grain of salt when people are, a) b) and c), and often will add that I need to learn the corporate world if I want to change it. But I don't think corporations are all bad. I think they are simply needing to be bettered but a superbly valuable asset to the culture of the states.

So, so what I'm a corporate law student. Get over it.

ARGUMENTS WITH FRIENDS OVER "CORPORATIONS"

I've had a few frustrating conversations with friends about corporations. I think so many people are anti-corporation, but they use all types of products and services from corporations. What an oxymoronic issue.

Yes, corporations can be evil, manipulative, poorly run, abusive, and all the like, but to totally ignore all the good things corporations do is somewhat ignorant. The products and services afforded to us by corporations are so intriguing, and I think many people miss the point that while corporations are often pieces of work, they also are (collectively) way important to the continued brilliance of people in this country and world. As Mike Moffatt for Thought Co. outlines:

> Large companies can supply goods and services to a greater number of people, and they frequently operate more efficiently than small ones. In addition, they often can sell their products at lower prices because of the large volume and small costs per unit sold. They have an advantage in the marketplace because many consumers are attracted to well-known brand names, which they believe guarantee a certain level of quality.[96]

So, corporations really run the gambit of good and bad (just like us humans). One might want to think about the absolute powerhouse corporations are in order to break them down and see what the actual benefit of them is, or rather, critique them. My mentor mentioned that corporations came up with the COVID-19 vaccine, so they definitely do some type of good, at least some of the time.

CORPORATIONS IN GENERAL

Corporations are often bad and evil in many ways. Think about things like Amazon working their employees to death, Walmart not paying its workers a livable wage, the countless number of fast-food jobs that don't allow people to make enough to house and feed themselves[97], etc.[98]

---

[96] Mike Moffatt. Corporations in the United States. Thought Co. (2020).

[97] Information from a general knowledge of companies with dangerous practices.

[98] There is also a plethora of articles that describe the evilness of corporations... Here are four of them:
https://www.tampabay.com/news/business/corporate/from-bad-to-baddest-the-ten-nastiest-corporations-of-the-moment/2295964/
https://www.cracked.com/pictofacts-2171-evil-things-huge-companies-have-done
https://slate.com/technology/2020/01/evil-list-tech-companies-dangerous-amazon-facebook-google-palantir.html

But companies also do a significant amount of good, which is hard to ignore. Amazon delivers much needed supplies to anyone in a matter of a few days (with a Prime subscription), Walmart allows people to shop for things at a massive discount, and we all love driving through fast-food places for our quick meals. There are certainly upsides and downsides to the nature of corporations.

As the Atlantic points out: "Large corporations are vilified in a way that obscures the innovation they spur and the steady jobs they produce."[99] The article continues on to point out many fascinating logical inferences about the way people feel about business (big and small) and the relative facts about corporations. One of the best points is that:

> In 2015, small enterprises were four times more likely to lay off their workers than large ones. Workers employed by large firms also earned more—on average, 54 percent more than workers at small companies. Companies with more than 500 employees offer 2.5 times more paid leave and insurance benefits and 3.9 times more in retirement benefits than workers at firms with fewer than 100 employees. Large firms are also more likely to be unionized, and they employ a greater share of women and minorities than small firms do, making Big Business an unlikely enemy of progressives.[100]

There are also, generally, good corporations out there. Hannah Durbin from the company *Classy* outlines nine in her article, and I touch on my favorite five[101]:

Google
Google, in many opinions does well because of its environmental awareness, treatment of employees,

---

https://www.thetoptens.com/most-evil-companies/
[99] Atkinson & Lind. Is Big Business Really that Bad? The Atlantic (2018).
[100] id.
[101] Hannah Durbin. 9 Socially Conscious Companies to Model This Year. Classy (2021).

and general contribution to the world. The company has been working on its carbon footprint (aiming to be carbon-free by 2030) and upping the awareness of other companies as it relates to their environmental impact. Finally, "[from] employee gift matching, to paid time off for volunteering, Google inspects nearly every part of their business with a social impact lens."[102]

Ben & Jerry's
As Durbin outlines:

> Ice cream tastes just a little sweeter when you know the makers work to promote safe, socially responsible ingredients and business practices. Since the 1980s, Ben & Jerry's has supported a number of important causes, many of which are directly tied to the business of making ice cream.[103]

Ben & Jerry's has fought against growth hormones used in cows, worked to encourage employees and others to better their communities, given social justice program grants, and fought against racism. "Ben & Jerry's impact is then further amplified by the Fairtrade social premium, an additional amount of money paid on top of the fair price that farmers receive."[104]

LEGO
LEGO is another company that is, at least, aiming toward some type of social awareness. Durbin details this saying:

---

[102] id.
[103] id.
[104] id.

The LEGO Group is one of the most notable examples of how social responsibility can be an incredible asset to a well-known brand... In September of 2020, the LEGO Group announced that they were set to invest $400 million over the next three years to support their social responsibility and sustainability efforts... by the end of 2025, they are going to start by phasing out single use plastic bags and installing additional solar panels on all factories... By 2022, the LEGO Group is also aiming to reach eight million children around the world annually with learning through play. In collaboration with the LEGO Foundation, UNICEF, Save the Children, and local partners, the team is working to scale up programs that give children the opportunity to develop life-long skills.[105]

Warby Parker

Warby Parker is famous for their "We'll send you 5 pairs to pick from" business model. Though, their social justice model is another great thing about them, as they also provide glasses to those that are in need.[106] Durbin adds to this idea stating:

> Through their Buy-A-Pair, Give-A-Pair program, Warby Parker makes a monthly donation to their nonprofit partners, such as VisionSpring, to bring prescription eyewear to people in developing countries. The company has distributed more than eight million pairs of glasses since its start in 2010. As of April 1, 2020, a portion of purchases will additionally go toward personal protective equipment and preventative health supplies for healthcare workers and communities in need.[107]

---

[105] id.
[106] id.
[107] id.

Microsoft

Microsoft is yet another shining example of a company dedicated to doing good in the world. Durbin outlines this saying:

> Microsoft changed the way the world works, studies, and plays with their computers and software. But their ambitions go far beyond the screen. The company... began its giving program in 1983 when the fledgling company raised $17,000 for charity. As their CSR web page explains, Microsoft's giving program has not only given time (employees in the U.S. volunteered more than 750,000 hours for nonprofits in 2020 alone), but also cash. In fiscal year 2020, the program raised over $221 million for nonprofits.

This list could have many more companies and many of them are indeed Top 9 or 10 material. Many companies do in fact do good for the world, though people certainly have a right to be skeptical.

Furthering the idea of corporate social responsibility, here is a link to the 2019 Aflac graphic (https://www.aflac.com/docs/about-aflac/csr-survey-assets/2019-aflac-csr-infographic-and-survey.pdf) that goes over many corporate social responsibility statistics and inferences that include:

- Purpose v. Profit
- Social/Business Impact
- Scrutiny & Forgiveness
- Generational Differences
- Expectations
- Bad Behavior
- Many Other Stats & Figures[108]

---

[108] Aflac. 2019 Corporate Social Responsibility Report. Aflac (2019)

Businesses being "good" or "bad" is a tough debate. Though, given the research, perhaps corporations are not the worst thing in the world (though they could be bettered of course).

GENERAL ARGUMENTS FOR CORPORATIONS

"Advantages of a corporation include personal liability protection, business security and continuity, and easier access to capital."[109]

Other advantages include:

Competition: Businesses spur competition in the world and keep the world "a turnin.'" The American Dream is built on the ideas of manifest destiny and competition, and that's what businesses seem to do/provide. [110]

Global Stability: Put frankly: the world is better off as a whole with business deals spurring global conversations, innovations, and the like. Many companies are multinational and thus might have employees all over the world working toward a similar goal. This is, arguably, beneficial for the world.[111]

People-Backed Corporations: Behind the corporation and its ideals is almost always a person or group of people. Investors, directors, employees, and owners all benefit from, and are usually the backbone of the corporation.[112]

---

[109] Skye Schooley. Pros and Cons of Forming a Corporation. Business News Daily (2020).
[110] Up Counsel. Corporate Personhood. Up Counsel (2021).
[111] id.

People are Protected: The limited liability of corporations makes it the company's problem, usually, rather than the direct employees or other members of the corporation. This is highly important for the sake of people being able to guide the business in a safe and sustainable manner.[113]

Inclusion in Society: People working for companies allows them to work, live, and thrive in terms of being in the world. Yes, there are lots of problems with this argument, but corporations clearly employ a ton of people worldwide and oftentimes enable them to live a better life than without a job.[114]

To add, *The Economist* writer K.N.C. gives these powerful things that would not exist without corporations:

> Without business we would not have:
>
> * Ships, trains, and cars
>
> * Electricity, lighting, and heating equipment
>
> * Most of our food supply
>
> * Most of our lifesaving pharmaceuticals
>
> * Clothes for our children
>
> * Our telephones and smartphones
>
> * The books we love to read
>
> * The ability to access, more or less immediately, so much of the world's online information
>
> And let's not forget your paycheck. "Meeting payroll," to invoke a now old-fashioned phrase, is nothing less than a heroic act.[115]

---

[112] id.
[113] id.
[114] id.

So, again, there are benefits to corporations.

GENERAL ARGUMENTS AGAINST CORPORATIONS

"Disadvantages of a corporation include it being time-consuming and subject to double taxation, as well as having rigid formalities and protocols to follow." (Business News Daily).

Other disadvantages include:

Businesses Being "Real": The weird conundrum that businesses are people, just not "natural" people is a distinction that is strange to many. The idea that a business is its own distinct person could easily be construed as disrespectful to actual people and in its most basic form: a lie for the sake of business.[116]

Lack of Morality: The lack of morality of corporations is often atrocious. This must be bettered in America in so many ways (pay, environmental-impact, treatment of employees, mental health time off).[117] My mentor sent me an article about a pregnant Amazon worker that lost her child duet to Amazon's condition. This is terrible, but often the typical nature of tough-to-work-for companies.[118]

---

[115] K.N.C. Why we should embrace big business. The Economist (2019).
[116] Up Counsel. Corporate Personhood. Up Counsel (2021).
[117] id.

[118] Lauren Gurley. Amazon Denied a Worker Pregnancy Accommodations. Then She Miscarried. VICE (2021).

Corporate Personhood is Silly in Many Ways: The analysis of this by Up Counsel is kind of funny but very true. They say:

> A big part of personhood is feelings. Businesses have no feelings because they are not people. A business can't live. It can't die. Businesses do not feel love, get married, or have children. If a business is not alive, then it is not a person and does not deserve personhood.[119]

Businesses are Money-Driven: Businesses (save nonprofits and social entrepreneurships, etc.) usually have a main (but not only) goal of making money. Thus, most businesses are money-driven and money-first, which often creates a lot of problems, especially in terms of immorality.[120] Amazon is yet another good ("bad") example here.

Corruption of Big Business: Big business can yield a ton of corruption, unjust enrichment, abuse of power, and the like.[121] Also, money corrupts people, and corporations are a prime example of such.

Environmental Damage: Corporations are known to damage the environments they are in, that is no secret at all, and is the reason for the plethora of regulations in industries. *Future of Working* provides this analysis on how corporations can be especially damaging to developing countries:

> Most developing countries do not have the same level of regulation and oversight that the developed world maintains to protect the environment. When these

---

[119] id.
[120] id.
[121] Future of Working. 19 Advantages and Disadvantages of Multinational Corporations. Future of Working (2021).

firms decide to do business in the international market, they are subject to local laws – not the ones that govern their domestic headquarters – when working to obtain raw materials.[122]

Obviously, environmental damage is a factor here.

Overworked Employees: Many companies overwork their employees. Personally, I worked as a tutor for a company that wanted us working a minimum of 25 hours a week, which is a lot of students and a ton of unpaid prep time, while I was a full-time student. I tried and tried to communicate to them, but it was brutal because they kept adding and adding students to my already overworked load.

High Stress & Low-Paid Work Environments: Both high stress environments and low-pay are significant downsides to corporations, who often profits to the general wellbeing of their employees. Many, many companies fall under this reasoning flaw.

A "CONSERVATIVE SOCIALIST" IDEOLOGY

I believe in the institutions: law, education, business, culture, etc. I am skeptical of how things are often run, accomplished, dealt with, etc. oftentimes, which is why I study all these subjects to hopefully better them throughout the things I do in my life.

I also believe that the institutions are meant to serve the people. If an institution doesn't work for people or for the benefit of people, I'm pretty skeptical of it. Institutions are for the betterment of people in my mind.

---

[122] id.

I consider that to make me a conservative socialist, red and light blue. Say what you want about it, but I think I acknowledge both sides of all these arguments pretty damn well.

CONCLUSION: BUSINESS IS THE HEARTBEAT OF AMERICA, JUST TO BE HONEST, BUT...

Business is the heart of America and American capitalism. My mentor/professor included the President Calvin Coolidge quote which reads: "After all, the chief business of the American people is business. They are profoundly concerned with producing, buying, selling, investing and prospering in the world."[123] That's the analogy I love to think of: businesses here, there, and everywhere, that's the states I know. Small business, medium-size business, large corporations: all pumping much-needed blood to the people in this country. Nonprofits are also considered corporations, so, as my mentor mentioned to me, there is likely a company that does something you absolutely love/support for every corporation you can't stand and/or hate. Personally, I honestly can't imagine the US without corporations or businesses; it'd be a different type of country without them. Corporations are problematic very often and have less support than we'd hope (a majority of the country, nearly 80%, is not confident in big business[124]), but even still, businesses are undeniably here to stay.

---

[123] Ellen Terrell. When a quote is not (exactly) a quote: The Business of America is Business Edition. Library of Congress (2019).

[124] id.

"Bitch! I'm that, I'm that, I'm that bi-bi-bitch
I don't ask for forgiveness or permission
If I want it I'mma fuckin' go get it
On the court all by myself no competition
Y'all be mad about me like I never listen
Uh, I'm the big boss; Uh, I be spillin' sauce
Uh, I've got no fear of fallin' off; Uh, y'all niggas too soft
I'm that bitch, I'm that bitch; I'm that, I'm that, I'm that
I'm that bitch, I'm that bitch; I'm that, I'm that, I'm that
I'm that bitch, I'm that bitch; I'm that, I'm that, I'm that
I'm that bitch, I'm that bitch; I'm that, I'm that, I'm that. Bitch"

-- Saweetie

"The 'Funding' Problem"

TABLE OF CONTENTS

INTRODUCTION: "MIDDLE-MAN MENTALITY"

THE ISSUE OF PAYING FOR A LAWYER AS A LAYPERSON

THE ISSUE OF NOT PAYING FOR A LAWYER

THE ISSUE OF CORPORATE PRO BONO

THE ISSUE OF LAW FIRM FUNDING (I.E., EQUITY FOR LAWYERS ONLY)

THE GENERAL ISSUE (OR NON-ISSUE OF LAW BEING DRIVEN BY   MONEY

CONCLUSION: "LOL FUNDING LAWYERS LOL"

"I went from the favorite to the most hated

How a bitch overpaid but still underrated?

Don't want no sympathy just know I changed

I'll be damned if the name the reason I don't make it

It contradicted what I stand for

The backlash ain't what I planned for

Now I know better, so I'm moving better

Ten toes to the damn floor"

-- Latto

INTRODUCTION: "MIDDLE-MAN MENTALITY"

I am, in this thesis, (mostly) just running you some of the facts (well, OK, a lot of the facts) about law. Take them as shallow, face-value, or deeper than meets the eye, but in the end, I'm arguably directly in-between nonlawyers and lawyers as a *nearly* Master of Legal Studies (smile). This perspective is quite obtuse and acute simultaneously: I know a good amount I can lay out for you, but I remain in the middle as to what I think and project (namely why I present problems rather than solutions).

This paper specifically is, thus, a very simple breakdown of the issue of funding in the legal realm: first, with a touch of insight into funding a simple 1 person, 1 lawyer contract, and furthering into issues of corporate pro-bono, the fact that law firms can ONLY be owned (as in hold equity) by lawyers[125], and the general issue of law being driven by men and money.[126] These issues are basically (as in easily) apparent and can be described in a few sentences each, which I find very alarming. That is all to say: I am just an MLS, but here are 5 major problems (described very briefly, but also very powerfully) I find with funding in terms of the law (take them as you will):

THE ISSUE OF PAYING FOR A LAWYER AS A LAYPERSON

Lawyers cost, on average, anywhere from $100-$1,000 an hour (which ranges from solo practitioners to corporate lawyers) if they're not working pro-bono (aka for free and for good cause) or on contingency (a fee assessed when the case is completed), as law school and the practice of law

---

[125] As my professor for this course noted, "Only lawyers can own equity in an entity for a law firm. This is because equity holders make decisions about how the firm will operate. Other friends/family can loan money to the law firm; they just can't have a voice in the decisions made by the firm, which means they can't be equity owners. Lawyers have ethical rules which constrain their conduct. Non-lawyers are not bound by these rules, so they can't be equity holders (decision makers) but they CAN loan money to the firm."

[126] More of a description of the money issue here though, as the male-driven aspect will be researched in much more depth in other papers—namely the "Leadership for Women in Law" papers.

are both expensive (as is the lawyer lifestyle) and student/business/etc. loans must be repaid. There are quite a few reasons why lawyers are expensive and are described in the other paper for this course ("The 'Law Firm' Problem). Often though, the choice of paying for a lawyer to represent you is a decision of whether to pay up (to the lawyer and his fees) or basically, lose.

THE ISSUE OF NOT PAYING FOR A LAWYER

So, you cannot pay a lawyer, which can often lead to 2 choices: defend yourself (aka "pro se") or find a pro-bono lawyer.[127] I will discuss the issue of pro-bono lawyers in the next section, but here is the issue of if you defend yourself: point blank, you'll be going against a lawyer who is probably well-trained in this specific field on both substantive law concerning the issue and the formalities of the legal system. Again, point blank, good fuckin' luck, 99 out of 100 times you're going to lose (an exaggeration here, but you get the point: going against a trained lawyer as a nonlawyer in a court of law... a spell for disaster). As a lawyer writing for LinkedIn writes:

> Your chances of winning your case are slim. Statistics show that pro se defendants typically lose. Thus, by the time a party (either criminal defendant or civil plaintiff/defendant) realizes they are in over their head, it is too late to backtrack and hire an attorney.[128]

---

[127] There are other choices like contingency fees and state-sponsored alternatives (as a professor noted to me) though.
[128] Jay Wampler. 7 Reasons Why You Should Not Represent Yourself

The lawyer you're challenging has 3 years of brutal law school, numerous years perhaps decades worth of experience in the field, and the joke that you're representing yourself against them. Again, good fuckin' luck. The judge even thinks you're a joke representing yourself, so God-speed padawan.[1]

THE ISSUE OF CORPORATE PRO-BONO

So, who is the major supplier of pro-bono lawyers?? Corporate entities and big law firms (by far), yay![129] That means that the pro-bono lawyer you got probably makes TONS of MONEY PER HOUR and is likely doing pro-bono helping you because it IS REQUIRED FOR PROMOTION BY THEIR FIRM, NOT BECAUSE THEY CARE ABOUT YOUR FUCKING CASE.[130] Seeing the issue with this at all? There are big, big problems here, but is totally allowed/apparent in the legal system and there doesn't seem to be very much done about it. Do they think these high-paid, corporate lawyers really care about you and your case, and whether or not you win (even if they're required by the Modern Rules to act competently

---

in Court. LinkedIn (2016).
[129] Staci Zaretsky details the massive amount of pro bono work big law put in in 2020, stating: It should be noted that at each firm listed, the average attorney performed 151.6 hours or more of pro bono work last year, and the Am Law 200 as a whole contributed about 5.453 million hours of pro bono work.
Staci Zaretsky. The Biglaw Firms Where Lawyers Did The Most Pro Bono Work. Above the Law (2020).
Eli Wald. Legal Profession Course. DU Sturm (2021).
[130] Knowledge gained from Professor Wald's "Legal Profession" course. DU Sturm (2021).

and pursue your objectives zealously)?[131]
Hmmmm…..

THE ISSUE OF LAW FIRM FUNDING (I.E., EQUITY FOR LAWYERS ONLY)

So, here's the main issue of law firm funding: only lawyers can hold equity in law firms and thus the "production of law". I.e., no one holding equity in a law practice is a nonlawyer. Equity holders make operation decisions and thus nonlawyers could not do this (apparently). Nonlawyers can loan money to a firm, but cannot be equity holders, as lawyers have rules of conduct that nonlawyers are not held to.[132]

I can let you dream up all the God-awful, or perhaps not-God-awful issues of "lawyers-only" equity of the issue of the law.

To add to this debate, only lawyers can practice law. MSLA's, MLS's, paralegals all can know the law: but cannot practice it. I cannot practice law despite writing this thesis: in fact, I have absolutely no right to if I don't pass the Bar in the state I want to practice in.[3]

Again, is this line of reasoning troubling you? I did, in fact, write this entire legal thesis, but cannot offer a lick of legal advice, or I could be sued (smile). Having trouble with this or no?

---

[131] ABA. Modern Rules of Professional Conduct Rules 1.1 and 1.2. ABA (2020).
[132] ABA. Modern Rules of Professional Conduct Rule 1.4. ABA (2020).

Perhaps nonlawyers will say yes to that and lawyers will not (smile).

This is a big debate in the legal field and some states have mobilized to test out "nonlawyer but law professional law practice". Much is left to be seen on this debate that features qualified legal people, but that are not truly lawyers. Letting them into more practice areas could be monstrously changing to the legal landscape. 5 states are either considering it or have implemented this type of practice for nonlawyer law professionals (those states being Arizona [implemented], California [exploring], Illinois [deliberating], New Mexico [deliberation], Utah [implementation].[133]

THE GENERAL ISSUE (OR NON-ISSUE) OF LAW BEING DRIVEN BY MEN & MONEY

Law is driven by money and men (which will be evidenced in other papers in this thesis). Men are more numerous and the higher earners in the field.[134] Little needs to be said after this long-experienced, worldwide, and very problematic issue. The money part is a problem because lawyers are among the wealthiest people in the world (individually and as a collective group) and they basically (not even basically, just generally and totally) write many of the rules of the world (my professor noted that many nonlawyers also write the rules too).[135] So, the rich(est) write the rules. It is

---

[133] Abra Coe. Where 5 States Stand on Nonlawyer Practice in Law Regs. Law 360 (2021).

[134] Jennifer Cheeseman. Number of Women Lawyers at an All Time High but Men Still Highest Earners. US Census Bureau (2018).

truly the biggest monopoly out, hell us laypeople can't even truly invest in this ridiculous system (because we're not lawyers and not held their rules). Again, see an issue with that? (Smile).[136]

CONCLUSION: "LOL FUNDING LAWYERS LOL"

Lol the funding issue. There's 3-5 at the very least (as described), and they're all a piece of work. This paper, especially the way it is so simply done and yet can be described as a MAJOR ISSUE OF THE LAW, is the exact reason why I wrote this thesis.

"You know what I came to do; you know what I came to do"

-- Chris Brown

"The 'Bartering of Powers & Parties' Problem"

TABLE OF CONTENTS

---

[135] Eli Wald. Legal Profession Course. DU Sturm (2021).
[136] As a counterpoint: my mentor who edited this work suggested that this is a big reason to not allow nonlawyer ownership, as it could result in a bunch of money-hungry investors messing up the system of law. This is a very valid point, though these are all theoretics as it largely hasn't happened in the US.

INTRODUCTION: "WHAT I LEARNED IN ECONOMIC ANTHROPOLOGY"

THE IDEA THAT BARTERING TAKES MANY FORMS & MUCH SOPHISTICATION, AND THAT NEGOTIATION & MEDIATION ARE COMPLEX ISSUES

THE ISSUE OF POWER IMBALANCES IN NEGOTIATIONS & MEDIATION

CONCLUSION: "ANOTHER WILD TOPIC OF THE LAW"

That wasn't funny but she laughed so hard, she almost cried
They're counting months they've been together, almost 49
He's making fun of how she acted 'round the holidays
She wears a ring but they tell people that they're not engaged

They met in class for metaphysical philosophy
He tells his friends, "I like her 'cause she's so much smarter than me"
They're having talks about their futures until 4:00 a.m.
And I'm happy for them (and I'm happy for them)

But I wanna feel all that love and emotion
Be that attached to the person I'm holding
Someday, I'll be falling without caution
But for now, I'm only people watching

-- Conan Gray

INTRODUCTION: "WHAT I LEARNED IN ECONOMIC ANTHROPOLOGY"

I took a fascinating class my first year of collegiate study (at Tulane), which was a 300 level Anthropology course entitled "Economic Anthropology".

The main thing I learned was that everything is, even still, just a bartering system.

I have this good (work) I trade for other goods (money) to fuel my life with goods (apartment, house, car, food, computer, phone, etc.).

Money is just a placeholder, we're still, in society, simply trading goods. I can do this you can do that: let's trade.

A crazy but very real, actual, and true concept.[137]

THE IDEA THAT BARTERING TAKES MANY FORMS & MUCH SOPHISTICATION, AND THAT NEGOTIATION & MEDIATION ARE COMPLEX ISSUES

In terms of relating that to negotiation and mediation: bartering can be very intricate and sophisticated.

There are a) levels b) modes c) ways d) procedures e) (loose) rules and f) madness. I took Negotiation & Mediation at DU and it's a wild topic!

Bartering takes many, many forms, certainly. In this work and in the fields, bartering, negotiation, and mediation are all superbly complex and difficult to master despite the seeming "easiness of topic."[138]

THE ISSUE OF POWER IMBALANCES IN NEGOTIATIONS & MEDIATION

---

[137] Professor Truitt. Economic Anthropology Course. Tulane (2011).
[138] Professor Parks. Negotiation & Mediation Course. University of Denver (2021).

Power imbalances in negotiation and mediation are critical and essential to know.

The other paper for this study of "Negotiation & Mediation" is a deeper analysis of this topic, but the need to mention this in any case relating to negotiation topics is certainly a must.

CONCLUSION: "ANOTHER WILD TOPIC OF THE LAW"

Negotiation and mediation (and arbitration) are—certainly—other wild topics of the law; the reasoning for this paper has backed itself 20+ times over, and this is no different.

"Spit yo game.. Talk yo shit.. Grab yo ghat.. Call yo clique!"

-- Notorious B.I.G.

"The 'Male-Driven Field' Problem"

TABLE OF CONTENTS

INTRODUCTION: "WOMEN COULD SOLVE LAW'S BIGGEST PROBLEMS"

GOOD LAWYERING & WHAT IT TAKES

A TROUBLED PATH FOR WOMEN, ESPECIALLY DIVERSE WOMEN

PERHAPS CHANGING THE LAW SCHOOL IS A GOOD PLACE TO START

DIVERSE WOMEN LAWYERS IN ALL FIELDS, TOO!

CONCLUSION: "THE WORLD NEEDS MORE QUALITY WOMEN LAWYERS"

"Yo, she fire
Brown skin, pretty brown eyes
Slim waist, but her hips kind of wide
Thick thighs, she about 5'5", or about 5'6"
Pretty tits sittin' high, legs crossed when she sit
Hair was hangin' 'bout an inch, then she cut it off (cut it off)
Eyebrows on fleek, can't rub it off, no pencil
Trap music in the Benz coupe, with the top down
No nigga, just a shih tzu

Bad bitch, she only smoke blunts with the glass tips
And she buy Chanel bags, just to put her cash in
Chanel thigh-high boots, stash the 380 (stash the 380)
Money on her mind
she ain't thinkin' 'bout no baby (she ain't thinkin' 'bout no baby)
We used to sing Ashanti
"Baby, baby, ba-baby-y"
Now her mood is, "Fuck you, pay me" (ooh)
Used to ride the bus (uh), now she wear a bust down (uh)
Now, it's a Clearport every time she touch down (uh)
When they throwin' shade, she just make a touchdown (score)
Scorin' on you hoes, she real life goals

Shorty got her own car and her own crib (own crib)
She don't take no handouts, she don't owe shit (ooh, ooh)
Shorty pay her own bills, buy her own drip (drip, drip)
I can't keep my hands off her, 'cause she so thick (ooh, ooh)
Bust her wrist down, baby, you the coldest (ooh, ooh)
She don't go deep, 'cause it ain't her motive (yeah, yeah)
She gon' push the drugs just to keep her loaded (oh-whoa)
Got it out the mud and I had to notice
Shorty ain't never need a nigga
Never, ever need a nigga for nothin' (never need a nigga for nothin')

-- Young MA

INTRODUCTION: "WOMEN COULD SOLVE LAW'S BIGGEST PROBLEMS"

Simply put, women have the power to solve law's biggest problems. Some of them, all of them, whatever they can muster.

White men have ruled law for so long and yet, women (women of all shapes, sizes, religions, colors,

etc.) could be the ultimate solution to the problems I have laid out throughout the entirety of this thesis; this paper explains why.

GOOD LAWYERING & WHAT IT TAKES

Good lawyering, according to the book, The Good Lawyer, includes the following elements:

Empathy

Courage

Willpower

Being Able to Value Others

Intuition & Deliberative Thinking

Realistic Thinking

Being Able to Serve Clients

Being Able to Pursue Justice with Integrity

Persuasiveness

Quality Seeking[139]

Do you see how women could do all that significantly better than men? Women are simply better at these qualities than men are, hands down.

A TROUBLED PATH FOR WOMEN, ESPECIALLY DIVERSE WOMEN

---

[139] Linder & Levit. The Good Lawyer. Oxford University Press (2014).

However, though quality women lawyers might be the exact solution the law needs, they serve to foster through a difficult path. This path is one that includes a fight for more women partners, which is an important marker of success. Partnership is important in law because it means power in a firm. Women need that power, and the world would truly benefit from them having that power. The "path to partnership" is outlined in a text entitled such, with the following elements:

 Getting Started at a Firm

 Beginning Full Time Law Practice

 Gaining Practical Skills

 Gaining Substantive Skills

 Maintaining Ethics & Professional Responsibility

 Time Management & Navigating Office Relations

 Criticism & Reviews

 Recruiting & Placement

 Business Development

 Partnership & Beyond[140]

A long process that can be troubled for women for many, many reasons, that include:

The Idea of "Women as Immigrants" in Law

Sexual Harassment & Harassment in General

Discrimination & Mistreatment in General

Dealing with Men (Especially Incompetent Ones)

---

[140] Steven Bennett. <u>The Path to Partnership</u>. Praeger (2004).

Having to Have the Confidence to "Play with the Boys"

Childcare & Being a Good Mother with Work/Life Balance

Showing Success & Being Ostracized for It[141]

Even still, women are redefining, reforming, and reshaping the law in a myriad of ways DESPITE these societal and legal issues.

PERHAPS CHANGING THE LAW SCHOOL IS A GOOD PLACE TO START

I was lucky, in my law school experience, to have female professors and mentors and the like. I am always fascinated at the strength and empathy women show and I know women seeing other women in powerful and meaningful positions is empowering, because I feel the same ways seeing black and queer people in the same light.

It is truly inspiring to see someone like you, and most all lawyers will have graduated from law school, so it seems intelligent to try and get more quality women professors and librarians and administrators in law school, again, for the betterment of all people (as empowering women does).

Unfortunately, women professors face many challenges that mimic those that women lawyers see, which includes:

Experiencing Legal Academia as Outsiders

Problems of Association & Isolation

Underrepresentation

---

[141] id.

> Only 7% of Law Faculty are Women of Color, Women are Only 34% of Full Time Professors, etc.

Barriers to Entry

> Role Models, Training, Intent/Awareness Norms, Hiring, Discrimination, Racism, Sexism, etc.

Ugly Truths

> Judgments, Lack of Others like You, Perceptions, Polarization, Labeling, Negative Treatment, Invisibility, Silencing, Sexual Harassment, etc.

Students

> Testing You, Disrespect, Confrontations, Toughness to Deal, Privilege at Institutions, Overburdening with Role Modeling, Bias with Evaluations, etc.

Promotions & Tenure

> Denials Despite Good Performance, Having to Sue, Teaching Barriers, Unrewarded Service, Publish or Perish Pressure, Fight or Flight Responses, etc.

Leading the Change

> Peculiar University Operations, Getting Intentional about Leadership, Obligations Felt, Bias & Discrimination, Antiracism, etc.

Work/Life Balance

Kids!, Workaholic Problems, Struggles, Gendered Expectations of Parenting, Complexities of Life, etc.[142]

Whole lot going on there huh.

The path for women is certainly tougher for men, but women are so important to the important changes we need in the states.

DIVERSE WOMEN LAWYERS IN ALL FIELDS, TOO!

Changing the "face" of law schools is good, but we also need more quality women lawyers in practice. Personally, I would love to see women dominate the field of law (what a breath of fresh air that would be).

If you're interested in the topic of women lawyers in the various fields of law, I recommend the book: *You Don't Look Like a Lawyer*, by Tsedale M. Melaku. It is a fascinating work that describes the issue of women lawyers (especially black women and women of color) are indeed marginalized in the field of law. Her masterful work discusses the extra labor black women and women of color do in the field of that that is not really billed or often related to work. [143]

Women of color have to work through so many difficult issues and it's not the justice we need.

---

[142] Holly English. Gender on Trial. ALM Publishing (2003).
[143] Tsedale Melaku. You Don't Look Like a Lawyer. Rowman & Littlefield Publishers (2019).

CONCLUSION: "THE WORLD NEEDS MORE QUALITY WOMEN LAWYERS"

Women can change a ton about the world. The world simply needs more quality women lawyers.

> "Stupid boy; I hate your guts (I hate your guts)
> Let's mess around; We'll make it rough
> You try to look; I see you dance
> You wear your heart; Inside your pants
> Stupid boy (stupid boy); Let's keep it clear
> That I decide (that I decide); When you come here
> You move around (you move around); And I do too
> I am so happy; That I'm not you (that I'm not you)
> Stupid boy; (Boy) stup-stup-stup-stupid
> Stupid boy; (Stupid boy)"
> --Slayyyter

"Head up and my heels high; That's what life suppose to feel like
Throw it back, throw it back now; For the '99 and the two thou'
Yeah, yeah, yeah, yeah

Girl you working with some ass yeah, you bad yeah; Make a nigga spend the cash yeah, his bag yeah
Girl you working with some ass yeah, you bad yeah; Make a nigga spend the bag yeah, his cash yeah
Girl you made it, you made it; Aw yeah, you made it, you made it
Baby girl you made it, you made it; Aw yeah, you made it, you made it

Self love is the best love, yeah, yeah
Self love is the best love, yeah, yeah

Self love is the best love, yeah, yeah
Self love is the best love, yeah, yeah

Ya made it, yeah, yeah
Oh yeah, yeah
Mmh yeah, yeah
Mm yeah, yeah"

-- Teyana Taylor

SOCIAL/POLITICAL
12. **Legislative Drafting – "The 'Written Law' Problem"**
13. **Intermediate Legal Analysis – "The 'Argument' Problem"**
14. **Remedies [Directed Research] – "The 'Just and Proper' Problem"**
15. **Contracts [Directed Research] – "The 'Contract Specifies' Problem"**
16. **Negotiation & Mediation – "The 'Settlement' Problem"**
17. **Trusts & Estates – "The 'Planning' Problem"**
18. **Education Law – "The 'School' Problem"**

19. Constitutional Law – "The 'Rights' Problem"

"The 'Written Law' Problem"

TABLE OF CONTENTS

INTRODUCTION

THE PROBLEM OF "LAWS ON THE BOOK"

THE PROBLEM OF REVISED & PERFECTED LANGUAGE

THE PROBLEM OF IMPLEMENTATION & ENFORCEMENT

THE PROBLEM OF THE PUBLIC AND REASONABILITY

CONCLUSION: "A LOT WRONG OR THAT CAN GO WRONG WITH THE LAW"

"If it's up,

Then it's up,

Then it's up,

Then it's stuck"

-- Cardi B.

INTRODUCTION

The law is written by the legislature: usually a collective of lawyers and some laypeople who draft the laws that people in the respective legislative bodies request. Senators and Congresspeople debate the laws as written and then a select few are amended (or not, which is rare) and passed into law.[144]

---

[144] Ideas used from Professor Whitlow's "Legislative Drafting" course at DU. DU (2021). The ideas in this paper largely reflect the ideas learned in the course and through study of the law as it is written.

The very first article of the Constitution gives the Legislative Branch this power to write the law.[145] There are federal and state laws to abide by, though there are many concerns, issues, and problems with the written law / writing law in general.

This paper introduces the issue of "the law on the books," various language issues, and the problems with the law being enforced/handled by the public.

THE PROBLEM OF "LAWS ON THE BOOK"

There's a ton of ways to approach this topic of the "laws on the book," but being a sociologist, I approach it in the sense of deviance; laws are meant to control deviance and allow for a more perfect society (as OK as we can be). Laws are meant to deter bad behavior and encourage good behavior, in a sense. Laws are meant to harmonize. Laws are social control and are a hope for the betterment of society.[146] Legislating things means either legalizing them, deterring them, criminalizing them, or incentivizing them usually. This places a lot of power and responsibility on those who write the laws. OK.

So here's the problem: laws have to be written that way, interpreted that way, and put into practice that way.

That requires: the legislature to write good and clear laws, the judicial system to interpret the laws well and in the meaning as they were intended, and citizens to act right (as in 1) obey the law to the extent you can 2) allow for discretion but acknowledge that laws are law).

How often do you think this gets fucked up? Like… a lot right? Yeah. That's the problem. I'm not suggesting a

---

[145] U.S. Constitution. Article I.
[146] Adler & Adler. <u>Deviance and Social Control</u>. Sage (2013).

different system than the legislature… but as Ab-Soul says: "you've got pro-gress, you've got Con-gress."[147] Literally so much can go wrong with written law that problematic occurences are almost expected.

THE PROBLEM OF REVISED & PERFECTED LANGUAGE

Because the law has this three-pronged (or four-pronged, including the executive check/extra offering of orders) pursuit of the legislative, the judicial interpretation, and society regulated there has to be pretty damn clear and pretty damn refined language. A mistake of a word, a comma, a phrase, a period even, could spark a dispute of the law. Legal writers who write US and state codes are well-trained in the art of writing language that is exact, refined, and well-stated (so as to avoid disputes of the law). Many do not realize that about the law as it is written and as it affects the public. Technicalities of the law happen all the time: and can be devastating.[148] Keep that in mind.[149]

---

[147] Schoolboy Q. Terrorist Threats. TDE (2013).

[148] One example comes from a George Washington Law Review article describes a curious error in a very well-known statute, the basic federal venue statute. The statute permits plaintiffs in federal civil cases to lay venue in "a judicial district where any defendant resides, if all defendants reside in the same state." 28 U.S.C. Section 1391(a)(1), (b)(1). It would seem obvious that, to lay venue based on this provision, a plaintiff must bring suit in some judicial district in the state in which all defendants reside. In fact, however, the article shows that, in some cases in which all defendants reside in the same state, this provision permits a plaintiff to lay venue in some other state. This perverse result was surely never intended by the statute's drafters; it is a drafting error.

Another example comes when the Virginia General Assembly accidentally repealed the exemptions of almost all industries from the statute requiring employers to allow employees not to work on Sabbath. (via Plan Sponsor article by Fred Schneyer).

THE PROBLEM OF IMPLEMENTATION & ENFORCEMENT

Laws are also needing to be implemented, enforced, and the like. This takes action from people like doctors, lawyers, police officers, landlords, and those who are responsible for the rights of others. Laws need to be observed more times than not, at least it seems, because they keep society in balance, people safe, and people on equal footing (if not a bad law). This, again, is a lot of power for people to hold. Those who write the law must be wise in implementation and enforcement intent, as this fuels society often. This is certainly something to keep in mind when considering the law as it is written. Some argue that "ridiculous laws are symptom of America's overcriminalization problem," which is backed by tons of evidence given racial injustice, the War on Drugs, and police brutality.[150] Others add to the argument saying that there are too many laws on the books.[151]

Police brutality is a general example that fits here. How many videos are there of cops abusing the law in some type of racialized/gendered/etc. expression of abuse of power. Enforcing the law is tough, and perhaps we need to find a better way to do it.

Again, more and more to consider about the written law and why it is problematized. I offer no suggestions here though, consistent with the thesis goals.

---

[149] Arthur Rynearson. Legislative Drafting Step-by-Step. Carolina Academic Press (2013).
[150] Michael Van Beek. Ridiculous Laws are Symptom of America's Overcriminalization Problem. The Hill (2020).
[151] Matt Stroud. The Problem With Our Current Legal System? Too Many Laws, Lawyers Tell Congress. Forbes (2013).

THE PROBLEM OF THE PUBLIC AND REASONABILITY

The public can run wild with poorly written/implemented/enforced laws, so the laws need to be written well and in a manner that a reasonable person would be able to follow them with little issue. My brilliant professor who edited this work noted that perhaps laws aren't meant as such in specialized industries, etc., which I would agree with. But, even still, I would argue that the bulk of laws are for people to be protected, etc. and accessible enough to be followed or at least worked through.

That is a large goal of legislative drafting and a very important one. Another point of consideration for the purpose of written law.

CONCLUSION: "A LOT WRONG OR THAT CAN GO WRONG WITH THE LAW"

Given all this: a lot about the law can go wrong. A lot. A lot is going wrong. Consider it.

"If it's up, then it's stuck,

Ain't no off switch"

-- Kash Doll

"The 'Argument' Problem"

TABLE OF CONTENTS

INTRODUCTION

THE "ANY ARGUMENT WITHIN THE RULES THAT WORKS" PROBLEM

THE DEVIL'S ADVOCATE PROBLEM

THE "EVIL LAWYER" PROBLEM

CONCLUSION: "LEGAL ARGUMENTS CAN AND ARE USED FOR EVIL, OFTEN"

"Last night I was swerving in the fast lane
Still kind of faded from my last drank
Sometimes I have nightmares 'bout my past days
If I'm dreaming let me sleep hope I don't crash mane
I feel like I'm dreaming
Somebody pinch me
I still can't believe it
I put my all in this and nothing came easy
I know God didn't bring me this far for no reason
I still can't believe it
I still can't believe it (I still can't believe yuh)
I still can't believe it naw (I still can't believe)

> I still can't believe it
> Still can't believe it naw (I still can't believe it ya)
> I still can't believe it; Still can't believe it naw"
>
> --- Drumma Boy

INTRODUCTION

This paper is a short (and sweet) analysis of the problem with "arguments in the law".[152][153]

THE "ANY ARGUMENT WITHIN THE RULES THAT WORKS" PROBLEM

Ok, so I told you that any argument within the rules and case law (and often public policy) is basically permissible. I hope you're getting where I'm going with this. You can get some "out there" arguments in the law. The idea of a "Devil's Advocate" is lowkey the basis of issues like prosecution, corporate law and the like. I would

---

[152] This paper is based on a DU course called "Intermediate Legal Analysis".
[153] Diane Kraft. Intermediate Legal Analysis Course. DU (2021).

know, half of my distinction at DU is in Corporate/Administrative Law.

It's crazy the arguments you "could make" and how that plays out in law study and practice. Oftentimes, there are no "designated" sides: you've got to argue everything. Can you win the argument on either side? And can you make a viable argument for both sides (i.e. both clients)? That's a helluva question. And it's a crazy problem of the law too.

THE DEVIL'S ADVOCATE PROBLEM

The problem with people being the devil's advocate is that they're, in effect, advocating for the Devil. Now, I'm not a super-holy person myself, but I have to say that there is somewhat of an issue with this. Perhaps in a criminal case, it is just that every person should be entitled to representation/an attorney no matter how heinous the crime, but even still the advocacy for civil and corporate issues is not this. It's problematic that lawyers can advocate for the worst of things in the name of client's interests. It's nuts and it affects everyone. Lawyers basically rule the states, so having them as an asset surely weighs the scales in your favor. Those with lawyers can manipulate the law to benefit them in ways that are insane (think of Amazon, Disney, and the like). We, as citizens (lawyers and nonlawyers alike), should be wary of these entities and the like using lawyers to be their devil's advocates. C'mon y'all, this is certainly a "problem of the law" and should be addressed in America for the benefit of all people.

THE "EVIL LAWYER" PROBLEM

The "evil lawyer" problem is thus evident and not needing to be explained in detail (look up jokes about lawyers online, you'll find material). Lawyers can use the rules (i.e. the client sets the objectives) to be a devil's advocate and manipulate the law in devious ways for their (likely powerful) client. This is an issue/problem of the law hands down.

But perhaps being a sociologist who evaluates people and a politician of sorts (insert politician jokes), I'm no better. But I know being a lawyer representing clients is not me, mostly because clients set the objectives and lawyers can run wild with this.

CONCLUSION: "LEGAL ARGUMENTS CAN AND ARE USED FOR EVIL, OFTEN"

So, basically, now you know. Legal arguments can be evil and are used for evil: and this is just a natural/normalized part of the lawyering process.

Again, this is a problem of the law.

"I could make a rich nigga chase

Pull that durag off, know I love fresh waves

Fat cheeks and a little bitty waist

East side nigga but he wanna be bae, okay

Bad bitch, gotta say it, like Short

Turn it over, put the ball in my court

Squat down, shit, I'm creasin' my forces

I get a nigga hooked, no chorus"

-- Saweetie

"The 'Just & Proper' Problem"

TABLE OF CONTENTS

INTRODUCTION: "THE LAW IS BUILT UPON THE IDEA OF REMEDIES"

    THE DEFINITION OF "REMEDY"

    THE DEFINITION OF "RIGHT"

TYPES OF REMEDIES (YES, IT'S MORE THAN JUST MONETARY)

WHY REMEDIES ARE SUPPOSED TO BE JUST AND PROPER

    THE PROBLEM WITH JUST AND PROPER

ADA LANGUAGE REGARDING RIGHTS & REMEDIES

THE EXAMPLE OF REMEDIES FOR DISABLED PEOPLE

CONCLUSION: "EVEN WITH REMEDIES, IT'S A COLD WORLD"

"She already winnin'

Now she workin' on her next win"

-- Young MA

INTRODUCTION: "THE LAW IS BUILT UPON THE IDEA OF REMEDIES"

Remedies relate heavily to and actually rely upon rights. Rights imposed upon call for remedies, which have a vast array of options for their purposes.[154] As Cornell Law points out: "A remedy is a form of court enforcement of a legal right resulting from a successful civil lawsuit."[155] Remedies, very often, also must be just and proper (i.e., a "fit") for the right that was infringed upon on (an important note). There are numerous problems with such.[156]

In addition, if a "right" is not wronged though, you have no claim for a remedy. The main issue of the "just and

---

[154] Tabb & Janutis. Remedies in a Nutshell. 3 Nutshell Series (2017).
[155] Cornell Law. Remedy. Cornell Law Legal Information Institute (2021).
[156] Richard Lapp. A Call for a Simpler Approach. University of Pennsylvania Journal of Labor and Employment Law (2001).Call for a Simpler Approach.

proper" nature of remedies, arguably.[157] The idea of "rights without remedies" is certainly a viable and proper counterargument to "no rights without remedies," which is also discussed in this work.[158]

The ADA gives rights and remedies to those with disabilities (namely the right to not be discriminated against for their disability). The ADA makes it so that accommodations that are "reasonable" and not an "undue burden" are a right, though those two terms are vastly debatable.

This paper discusses the idea of "remedies" and the essence of what they are/mean, giving broad (though often shallow for brevity) examples that explain the concept of remedies and then give more a specific (and depth having) example of the issues with accommodations in terms of the ADA. I thus start with a definition of "remedy" and correspondingly of "right" (in the US American sense), and then venture into the topic of the problematization of remedies, including an analysis of certain legal situations where "rights" and "remedies" are very much in question in terms of validity of treatment by the law.

Remedies are expansive, quintessential to the law, and yet, not as equitable as one would hope or expect. Remedies are troubled and could be fixed for the better with better doctrines (such as "equitable action" rather than "just and proper").

THE DEFINITION OF "REMEDY"

The four main types of remedies are: coercive, damages, restitution, and declaratory relief.[159] **Coercive**

---

[157] Tabb & Janutis. Remedies in a Nutshell. 3 Nutshell Series (2017).
[158] id.

remedies are mostly injunctions and specific performance, namely: "The requirement that a person perform, or refrain from performing an action."[160] **Damages remedies** are the most common remedy and are a fair compensation of loss for breach of contract and other issues.[161]

Restitution remedies are those that restore property to its rightful owner and disgorging of unjust enrichment of defendants. This is a remedy more focused on punitive actions based on the need to return or refund for property to another party. The purpose is to instill in the defendant's mind their responsibility to the justice of the plaintiff via compensation or return of property.[162] **Declaratory relief remedies** are a remedy that obtains a declaration of rights as the result of a "justiciable controversy" which occurs when the plaintiff is in doubt of their legal rights. This may not always be offered though.[163]

In addition, third parties' interest, the public, and various courts are relevant in remedies. Practicality of the entire process is another issue.[164]

Remedies are expansive and are the main reason for the practice of law: as suits and cases result in types of remedies for people (and yes, quite very often, the remedies given are monetary, though this is certainly not the only option in terms of remedies people have available to them when they go to court against another party).[165]

---

[159] Tabb & Janutis. Remedies in a Nutshell. 3 Nutshell Series (2017).
[160] Norm Mullen. The Contempt Law Has Changed. Department of Environmental Quality (2002).
[161] George Turnbull. What Remedies are Available for a Breach of Contract. Legal Vision (2020).
[162] Moore & Schneider. 16B PAPRAC § 31:16. West's(R) Pennsylvania Practice Series (2020).
[163] Cornell Law School. Declaratory Relief. Cornell (2021).; Tabb & Janutis. Remedies in a Nutshell. 3 Nutshell Series (2017).
[164] id.

There is an another and further breakdown of various types of remedies which is given in a subsequent section named for such. Remedies have a lot of subsections that are relevant in terms of discussion. Though, first, the definition of right is intricately tied to the definition of remedy and thus follows in the next section. Definitions are key to understanding these terms. Rights and remedies are both somewhat narrowly constructed in definition, though the language is spark for confusion, doubt, misunderstanding, and the like. "Rights & Remedies" is indeed a tough topic.

THE DEFINITION OF "RIGHT"

A right, according to West's Encyclopedia of American Law, is:

> In an abstract sense, justice, ethical correctness, or harmony with the rules of law or the principles of morals. In a concrete legal sense, a power, privilege, demand, or claim possessed by a particular person by virtue of law.[166]

Thus, rights can be abstract or concrete, which makes them very tough to comprehend if not a basic right such as life. I've always struggled with the idea of a right and what it means "to have a right to do something". I think it's tough to evaluate what people do and do not have the right to do (again, exploring that topic in my Constitution Law papers), but because these things we call "rights" are so debatable many people go overboard or way miss the mark by under-utilizing rights that the idea of rights should certainly be explored deeply in the study of law in terms of a social sense.

---

[165] Tabb & Janutis. Remedies in a Nutshell. 3 Nutshell Series (2017)
[166] West's Encyclopedia of American Law, Right. 2 The Gale Group, Inc. (2002)

Rights are given by the virtue of law and may be derived from (1) a statute, (2) common law, or (3) the Constitution.[167] The Constitution gives people the right to life, liberty, and the pursuit of happiness; numerous (though somewhat limited) civil rights; and other rights like press, remaining silent, a fair trial, counsel, etc. All in all, rights are pretty awesome though could be furthered.[168]

The ADA is a pivotal study in terms of rights. The ADA clearly reads:

> The ADA prohibits discrimination on the basis of disability in employment, State and local government, public accommodations, commercial facilities, transportation, and telecommunications. ... To be protected by the ADA, one must have a disability or have a relationship or association with an individual with a disability"[169]

Keep that prohibition of discrimination in mind.

TYPES OF REMEDIES (YES, IT'S MORE THAN JUST MONETARY)

Remedies may be classified in perhaps several (or more) ways, including civil, cumulative, judicial, legal, and provisional.[170]

Administrative law describes that, remedies are to be "set aside" with unlawful actions and thus give a highly broad definition of what can be a remedy.

> The APA, § 706(2), empowers a court to "hold unlawful and set aside" agency action that falls short of the various listed review standards. In a general sense, this is remedy language,

---

[167] Tabb & Janutis. Remedies in a Nutshell. 3 Nutshell Series (2017)
[168] US Constitution.
[169] ADA. A Guide to Disability Rights Law. ADA (2020).
[170] Legal Dictionary. Remedy. The Free Dictionary (2021).

but the phrase "set aside" should not be too narrowly construed. Thus, a variety of remedies are available.[171]

The phrase that stands out is "set aside agency actions". That is quite a phrase and could mean so many things in terms of what a remedy could possibly be. "Set aside" could mean all types of accommodations are truly lawfully necessary for places like schools, offices that employ people, and the like.

I think it is important to note that while some sources list only 3-4 major categories, the idea of types of remedies is certainly more expansive in the legal sense (and even more so in the general sense of what a remedy can be—medicinal, self-care, personal, herbal, situational, etc., etc.).

Remedies are indeed complex and certainly more expansive than simply a monetary transfer of funds for damages.[172]

WHY REMEDIES ARE SUPPOSED TO BE JUST AND PROPER

Legal remedies, quite often, are meant to be "just and proper" (in many state jurisdictions) because it is "fair" to both sides of the argument. Issues like injunctions to prevent activity (such as an injunction to stop a stalker from

---

[171] United States District Court, E.D. Pennsylvania. Comite de Apoyo a los Trabajadores Agricolas v. Solis. (2013).

[172] Wrapping one's head around the idea of rights and remedies is certainly a difficult task; it is actually one that I have been attempting to understand since taking American Government courses at HarvardX in 2018, and I'm still struggling through the idea of rights. It's really interesting to see what people think is a right and their respective reasoning for why (whether it be the Constitution, "God-given", "self-given", etc.).

being around someone, even if the case is still in question), damages (for things that violated someone's rights), unjust enrichment (like punitive damages for actions against a defendant that enriches the plaintiff in an unjust way), and other topics spring out from this idea.[173] The "just and proper" approach gives light to both sides of an issue and takes into the relative ability to perform the various remedies, etc. in question. Whether or not it is an excuse to do less for the "harmed" is a certainly a debate I make note of in this paper specifically.[174]

Case law explores issues of things such as labor law, criminal law, family law, patent law, corporate law, divorce law, and a lot of other types that explain how "just and proper" as a bar for remedies is often not as "justice-driven" as other bars in other jurisdictions such as "remedial purpose" and "equitable action". The basic idea here is that "remedial purpose" or "equitable action" would thus allow a judge to have more discretion with injunctions, damages, restitution, (reparations), etc.[175]

"Remedial purpose" and "equitable action" seem more just in many senses and in many cases and could possibly improve the justice system in many ways. The sources referenced in the previous paragraph discuss that these forms could be more just as they allow for an inclined ability to provide remedies to people without the worry of a need to be "just and proper" to the other side. Wrongs are

---

[173] Tabb & Janutis. Remedies in a Nutshell. 3 Nutshell Series (2017); Information from general understanding of law as a Pre-Law student while doing my undergraduate degree in Tulane, ULV, and USC.
[174] Tabb & Janutis. Remedies in a Nutshell. 3 Nutshell Series (2017).; Information from general study and understanding of remedies.
[175] Richard Lapp. A Call for a Simpler Approach. University of Pennsylvania Journal of Labor and Employment Law (2001).; William Briggs. Deconstructing "Just and Proper". Michigan Law Review Association (2011).

wrongs and thus that would lead one to believe that the former two types would take precedence over the latter one. This paper gives multiple examples of how "just and proper" is often too high of a bar for the judicial system providing remedies for people with issues of the law and is certainly an issue of the law.

THE PROBLEM WITH JUST AND PROPER

"Just and proper" as a legal bar is a lot higher to adjust to than "remedial purpose" or "equitable action." The mind runs wild with ideas here (corporations paying smaller fines than they should, banks not small businesses being bailed out, etc.), but personally, I think of educational issues like disability where "just and proper" for all students makes it a lot harder to justify things like various disability accommodations, as opposed to providing such things as a "remedial purpose" or "equitable action" initiative.

The language and connotation/denotation around the latter two forms of justice is a lot more conducive to a disabled student's development throughout their high school or collegiate or secondary education. As much as 2/3 of disabled students do not graduate from college despite matriculating.[176] This is certainly related to the idea that the law is not as helpful as it could be to disabled students because it's more built on what is just and proper rather than what is the correct remedy and what is equitable. My hope is that the legal world gravitates more toward justice than "just and proper" as this is, again, certainly an issue the law needs to consider in a thoughtful and complete manner. It is vastly important.

---

[176] Brennen Carter. Getting Ready Excessively. Brennen Carter (2020).

ADA LANGUAGE REGARDING RIGHTS & REMEDIES

The ADA (Americans with Disabilities Act) states in clear language that:

> **Individuals with disabilities continually encounter various forms of discrimination**, including outright intentional exclusion, the discriminatory effects of architectural, transportation, and communication barriers, overprotective rules and policies, failure to make modifications to existing facilities and practices, exclusionary qualification standards and criteria, segregation, and relegation to lesser services, programs, activities, benefits, jobs, or other opportunities.[177]

They the law lays out how disabled people cannot be discriminated against, save if the accommodation is an "undue hardship," stating:

> (b) Construction. As used in subsection (a) of this section, the term **"discriminate against a qualified individual on the basis of disability" includes**
>
> (5) **(A) not making reasonable accommodations to the known physical or mental limitations of an otherwise qualified individual with a disability who is an applicant or employee, unless such covered entity can demonstrate that the accommodation would impose an undue hardship on the operation of the business of such covered entity; or (B) denying employment opportunities to a job applicant or employee who is an otherwise qualified individual with a disability**, if such denial is based on the need of such covered entity to make reasonable accommodation to the physical or mental impairments of the employee or applicant.[178]

The ADA also discusses what accommodations can look like, stating:

> **(9) Reasonable accommodation. The term "reasonable accommodation" may include (A) making existing

---

[177] 42 U.S.C. § 126. 12101 (2018).

[178] 42 U.S. Code § 12112 (b)(5) (2018).

> **facilities used by employees readily accessible to and usable by individuals with disabilities; and (B) job restructuring...** [179]

As an educator, architect, employer, and the like, the hope from the disabled community is that you *make "reasonable accommodations" for disabled people, save (but also, even) when it is an "undue hardship"*. Though, the covered entity is the one that cannot discriminate, the individual teacher, employer, etc. is not sued, rather the school or the business.[180] In addition (which has been discussed), that last phrase is a Catch 22 and makes the ADA language consistent with the "just and proper" sentiment. As stated, the words, undue hardship mirror the term proper, as the words reasonable accommodations mirrors the term just.

See the issue here?

The ADA also talks about discrimination in public accommodations, stating:

> (A) **Discrimination**. For purposes of subsection
>
> (a) of this section, **discrimination includes**
>
> **(i) the imposition or application of eligibility criteria that screen out or tend to screen out an individual with a disability or any class of individuals with disabilities from fully and equally enjoying...**
>
> **(ii) a failure to make reasonable modifications in policies, practices, or procedures, when such modifications are**

---

[179] 42 U.S. Code § 12111(9) (2018).

[180] ADA National Network, What is a Public Accommodation under the ADA? ADA National Network. Title III of the Americans with Disabilities Act (ADA) prohibits discrimination on the basis of disability in the activities of public accommodations. Public Accommodations are considered to be businesses including private entities that are open to the public or that provide goods or services to the public.

> necessary to afford such... unless the entity can demonstrate that making such modifications would fundamentally alter the nature of such goods, services, facilities, privileges, advantages, or accommodations;
>
> (iii) a failure to take such steps as may be necessary to ensure that no individual with a disability is excluded, denied services, segregated or otherwise treated differently... unless the entity can demonstrate that taking such steps would fundamentally alter the nature... or would result in an undue burden...[181]

Again, very clear language here describing discrimination of disabled people. But, the "just and proper" type provisions ("undue burden," "fundamentally altering the nature of such") make it a debate for the ages among a plethora of disabled people at a ton of differing schools, workplaces, and environments.[182] The terminologies are so debatable how could it not be a debate? Various sections of the ADA contain this arguable language and it is a problem for people in the disabled community. Just and proper is indeed very similar to just for the disabled save when it is unproper for the employer, school, etc., which is basically what the phrase "undue burden" does.

This is clearly another certain problem of the law.

Though, sources give a description of the remedies under the ADA in decent detail. As Shegerian & Associates explain:

> Employees who successfully file disability discrimination claims have several remedies available. These include back pay, front pay, attorney's fees and costs as well as injunctive and affirmative relief like reinstatement.[183]

---

[181] 42 U.S.C. § 12182 (2018).

[182] id.

[183] Sherigan & Associates. What are the remedies of a disability discrimination claim? Sherigan & Associates (2016).

For students, schools are "required to make reasonable changes in its practices and policies to avoid discrimination and to afford children with disabilities an equal opportunity to participate unless doing so would impose an "undue burden."[184] In terms of public accommodations, discrimination claims from disabled people can render specific performance, monetary damages, punitive damages, and judicial consideration (i.e., the judge has discretion to do what they choose about the case).[185] After researching remedies available for students, there seem to be less remedies available for students than employees, but specific performance (accommodations, services, etc.) and injunctions (making schools stop unfair practices and implement better ones) seem like a good enough fix to be honest and are commonly known as a way to accommodate students with disabilities. Though, again, there are issues with this, especially considering the number of accommodations that don't get filled yearly by employers and schools (as a disabled person who has heard some disability horror stories, I can only imagine how high this number is).

THE EXAMPLE OF REMEDIES FOR DISABLED PEOPLE

The issue of "reasonable accommodations" for disabled people, both in school and in the workplace, is an issue of rights and remedies that spells out the issue of both well. Given the Americans with Disabilities Act (ADA), disabled people are entitled to reasonable accommodations in school and the workplace and other environments that people persist in.[186]

---

[184] American Diabetes Association. Americans with Disabilities Act. American Diabetes Association (2021).
[185] U.S.C. Sec. 12188 (2018).
[186] id.

Though, while disabled people may have a right to reasonable accommodations, as to what is reasonable or conversely, an "undue hardship" is a debate for the schools and workplaces (who hold a good amount of power in this situation), allowing them to skirt by with minimal accommodations based on legal and linguistic arguments of what is "reasonable" or "undue". Basically, semantics allow the entities to "only do what is reasonable" or "not allow accommodations" due to it being an 'undue burden,'" as that is "just and proper" for both sides. Again, with "remedial purpose" or "equitable action" this might be a bit of a different story—as the same with wealthier schools that can afford to provide better accommodations for their students, such as guide dogs, notetakers, power wheelchairs, accessible classrooms and the like.[187]

This argument around what is "reasonable" to the school means that while a student (i.e., think of a deaf or blind student needing certain accommodations to make school viable for them for what is often a 4-year or longer time) may have a right to accommodations at one school, they may not have that same remedy at a different school given the school's idea of what is reasonable. Accommodations (and services) like guide dogs, professors' notes, notetakers, wheelchairs, accessible buildings and other campus facets, etc., could all be debatably "an undue burden" on the school.[188]

A case study of a blind student who needed accommodations for medical school had the following to say about how he had to get creative to get through medical school. He states these conclusions about his case study of accommodations, stating:

---

[187] Brennen Carter. <u>Getting Ready Excessively</u>. Brennen Carter (2020).
[188] <u>id.</u>

1. Students are often the best source for information about accommodation strategies.
2. Accommodation needs can vary from one setting to another and may not be constant over time.
3. Students with disabilities can be very independent if they have the proper equipment and resources.
4. Academic departments and support offices (e.g., disability services offices) need to be very flexible and have access to resources to quickly respond to accommodation needs.
5. Timeliness of the accommodation may be particularly important for fast-paced, advanced, technical, or professional programs, including health and allied health programs where there is a required sequencing of courses.[189]

I, as a schizophrenic student, can confirm that these are valid conclusions.

A personal example from my life is that I went to USC where I could have a or be a notetaker (I both got notes and took notes for others), but at UW (and I think DU too) I did not and do not have that as an option. It is a debate as to whether students have a right to certain accommodations, but the ADA language of "reasonable" and an "undue hardship" is similar in stature to the language of "just and proper," and thus schools have the discretion to provide basically what they can and want, not what students actually need.[190]

The U.S. Department of Justice describes the peculiar nature of accommodations for people who are deaf, blind, or speech-afflicted (this time a secondary education example). They state:

---

[189] Javier. Javier and Medical School: A Case Study on Accommodations for Visual Impairments. University of Washington DO-IT (2021).

[190] Information from knowledge as a student in both undergraduate and graduate realms (2021).

What types of aids or services could be required for students?

There are no categorical rules. A school must assess the needs of each individual.

For a student who is deaf, deaf-blind, or hard of hearing, some examples are: exchange of written materials, interpreters, note takers, real-time computer-aided transcription services (for example, CART), assistive listening systems, accessible electronic and information technology, and open and closed captioning.

For a student who is blind, deaf-blind, or has low vision, some examples are: qualified readers, taped texts, audio recordings, Braille materials and refreshable Braille displays, accessible e-book readers, screen reader software, magnification software, optical readers, secondary auditory programs (SAP), and large print materials.

For a student with a speech disability, some examples are: a word or letter board, writing materials, spelling to communicate, a qualified sign language interpreter, a portable device that writes and/or produces speech, and telecommunications services.[191]

Remedies are available for students, but equity issues and other issues like "just and proper" and "not having an advantage over other students" and "no categorical rules for accommodations" still hold disabled students back.

Another example, in a larger scope than the ADA, that relates to disabled people is healthcare and whether or not accessible medicine prices (medicine being a remedy for illness/disability/general health) are a right. Personally, I've had medicine that, without insurance, would've cost me a retail price of upwards of $3,000 for a one-month-lasting shot (with Obamacare in California the shot was free though, which was amazing to see bills of $3,000 marked down to $0).

---

[191] Department of Justice. Meeting the Communication Needs of Students with Hearing, Vision, or Speech Disabilities. DOJ (2021).

I needed that medicine and arguably have a right to healthcare, but when I moved to a different state and didn't have the same access to healthcare insurance due to SSI being slow about responses, I was faced with tough questions. The main one being, should I 1) somehow find a way to pay $3,000, 2) don't take the medicine, or 3) hope something else would work? This was the beginning of my education graduate school experience and luckily the third option worked (I'm pretty stable and a fighter, especially with new meds), because Lord knows those are not ideal options. The remedy I needed, I kind of lost a right to by moving to a different state.

Did I have a right to the medicine? Maybe in one state and time, but certainly not in another state after switching in a short period of time. It's the same thing as the accommodations I got in grad school at UW and DU as opposed to USC. The "reasonability" and "just and proper" aspects of the law certainly cause issues for people like me.

See the problem with all this? Remedies and rights could be more than what they currently are if remedial purpose or equitable action was the basis of remedies rather than just and proper.

CONCLUSION: "EVEN WITH REMEDIES, IT'S A COLD WORLD"

Remedies require an infringed upon right, which is a problematic definition. Some rights have no accessible remedy and are thus "not a true right". Again, you can see the problem with this, potentially. In addition, the law also does not give access to many rights we as (perhaps more liberal or socialistic) people think we should have (the right to health/healthcare, the right to food, the right to a place to live, etc.) and possibly could make an argument that there is indeed a remedy for (Obamacare, free lunch programs and food banks, free housing, etc.).

Again, more problems of the law.

To be honest, I think the idea of "no right without remedy" is idiotic of lawyers to believe. So many things are a) not a right but there is an accessible remedy, as discussed and b) there are totally things without remedies though should still be considered a right. Perhaps these are moral rights rather than legal rights, but they are still needing to be acknowledged.

One harsh example I think of is if someone who is mentally ill and poor destroys another person's million-dollar mansion (either by intention, involving criminal aspects, or unintentionally somehow) the house owner for some reason does not have insurance (which, is problematic because he arguably has a responsibility to) on but certainly has a right to own/have/enjoy; and, the person who did the destruction can not pay the debt for the damages: I think the owner of the mansion clearly and definitively should have a remedy (which he does, it is just not really enforceable given the defendant's income bracket) for their destroyed home even if that poor person can not pay them back. (Go wild with thinking of more things that could easily have an accessible remedy but may not be a right—fair pay, retirement at a reasonable age, a decent family.)

So yeah my true thoughts are such and I think that explains why the second paper for this course talks about the idea of reparations as a culturally healing affair despite the fact that a) they're not necessarily granted a right given that black people are not enslaved people today (though certainly suffer its repercussions, which is certainly a valid argument in terms of progressive ideologies) and b) black people should certainly have a means of righting past wrongs despite there not being an exact monetary or other value that could equate for the pain/suffering/sorrow of being a black person in America, especially given the history of racism in this country.

_____
_____

"I'ma walk on stage with a whole 'lotta wata'!!!; With a whole 'lotta drip on me."

-- YoungBoy Never Broke Again

"The 'Contract Specifies' Problem"

INTRO: "I AIN'T READ SHIT, I AIN'T EVEN OK IN MY MIND; SO, THE CONTRACT I 'SIGNED'"

THE DEFINITION OF A CONTRACT

    FORMATION, "STATUTATION," INTERPRETATION, & NEGOTIATION

    PERFORMANCE & REMEDIES; RIGHTS & RESTITUTION

    MODIFICATIONS, BENEFICIARIES, & BENEVOLENCE

    DUTIES & DISCHARGE

    ADDENDUMS, AMENDMENTS, & ALTERNATIVE DISPUTE RESOLUTION

WHY CONTRACTS CAN BE PROBLEMATIZED

THE CONTRACTS WE SIGN DAILY

CONCLUSION: "THIS IS WHY PEOPLE FANTASIZE ABOUT CONTRACTS WITH THE DEVIL; PEOPLE WILD"

"I'll never be picture perfect Beyonce; Fly like J-Lo or
singing Baby like 'Shanti
I barely comb my hair, yeah, that's on a good day; I don't
care what the hood say
I ain't street like Keyshia, ain't never tried to be; And I got
soul in my soul but not quite like Mary; Ain't nothing really
R&B about me; And I say bump what the hood say

I'm sorry I ain't in the Benzes in my videos

I'm sorry I ain't even really trying to match my clothes
I can tell you paid a figure for McQueen dibs; But I can
also tell you who the King dealer is
And I got knowledge if you really want to talk about it; No,
I don't trust the crowd just to walk around it
So I'm writing the letter to the industry

It says "Fuck you, signed sincerely"

Aww, yeah
Here we go again
Solo, can you tone it down? Be more like them
But everything I'm not makes me everything I am

Aww, yeah
Ooh, here we go again
People talking shit but when the shit hits the fan
Everything I'm not makes me everything I am"

-- Solange

INTRO: "I AIN'T READ SHIT, I AIN'T EVEN OK IN MY MIND; SO, THE CONTRACT I 'SIGNED'"

So, the first thing I think of when I think of contracts are 2 things: 1) the crazy amount/specifications of contracts we sign daily and 2) student loans.

Thus, I'm going to talk about how we all sign these contracts, but whether or not a lot of the said contracts would really hold up in court; and, of course, the issue of a contract with such a ridiculous price for a much-needed good (i.e., college tuition). These issues put us all in a place of where we should consider whether the financial aid contracts we sign should truly be honored to their fullest extent, or rather something flexible that could be modified at any time.

Keep this in mind while reading this particular paper of this thesis: 1) the ridiculousness of contracts we sign daily 2) the extremity of college loans 3) the idea of being disabled/vulnerable while signing these contracts 4) the potential remedies for unfair contracts.

THE DEFINITION OF A CONTRACT

Simply, a contract is "a promise or set of promises for the breach of which the law gives a remedy, or the performance of which or some combination of words or conduct."[192]

It is important to acknowledge two main notes about contracts: 1) a promise is "a commitment or an undertaking that some event will or will not occur in the future.[193] A promise may be made by using express words (oral or written), or it may be implied from conduct or some combination of words and conduct." 2) a contract is only valid if both parties meant and intended to be legally bound by such contract.[194]

These are important to note, in terms of the problematization of contracts, as a promise could be many things, but whether or not the person promising or being promised is intending to be legally bound to that promise is a whole issue.

I continue this analysis of mostly definitions (and finishing with insights) of a "bit" of the problematizations of contracts, in terms of the law.

FORMATION, "STATUTATION," INTERPRETATION, & NEGOTITATION

I'm just going to give brief/loose definitions here for brevity. This is all simple contract law:

Formation – Bar Prep Hero provides a definition here:

> The legal formation of a contract generally requires an offer, acceptance, consideration, and a mutual intent to be bound. Each party must have capacity to enter the contract and it is said that the parties must have a "meeting of the minds."[195]

---

[192] Rowher et. al. <u>Contracts in a Nutshell.</u> Nutshell Series (2017).
[193] <u>id.</u>
[194] <u>id.</u>

It is important to note that an offer requires elements (from Fortune Law):

> It must be specific, complete, capable of acceptance, and intended to be bound by acceptance. It can be express or implied by conduct. It can be made to an individual or a group or persons. It can even be made to the world (such as in the famous case of Carlill v Carbolic Smoke Ball Co [1893] 1 QB 256, where an advertisement in the Pall Mall Gazette was held to be an offer).[196]

"Statutation" -- By "statutation" I mostly mean the statute of frauds. Simply put, this phrase is: "a generic term that refers to statutes which require that certain classes of contracts be in writing and signed by the party against whom enforcement is sought (often referred to as the "party to be charged")".

It is also important to note here that oral agreements are not void, though written contracts are a) more recognized, b) more official, c) more legally sound, and d) safer.

Interpretation – Interpretation is all about how contracts are read and determined to be "worded," "phrased," or "meant. The state where I am studying, Colorado, notes that, in terms of contract interpretation:

> Words or phrases not defined in a contract should be given their plain, ordinary, and generally accepted meaning.

---

[195] Bar Prep Hero Staff. Contract Formation. Bar Prep Hero (2021).

[196] Fortune Law Staff. Back To Basics – The Formation of A Contract. Fortune Law (2012).

> 1. When the court has determined the contract term is ambiguous or there is an oral contract where the terms are in dispute, contract interpretation is a jury issue and this instruction should be used.[4]

This means that if your contract doesn't have clear language (and probably definitions too): the jury could be deciding your terms. Keep this in mind with contracts.

Negotiation – As a book on contract negotiating states:

> Negotiating is a dynamic process of adjustment by which two or more parties, each with their own mutually conflicting objectives, confer together with the intention of reaching an agreement which at least satisfies their minimum needs on a matter of common interest.[197]

A discussion of what benefits your party and their party best in a deal: that's negotiation.

PERFORMANCE & REMEDIES; RIGHTS & RESTITUTION

More definitions for general understanding here:

Performance – Contracts involve promises, duties, and conditions that all have to be followed by both the supplier and the buyer. Any diversion from such could result in a suit for a breach of contract.[198]

---

[197] P.D.V. Marsh. Contract Negotiation Handbook. 3 Gower Publishing Inc. (2001).

Thus, performance is: "an analysis of the legal duties that become due under a contact, with special concern for when a given duty to perform will arise and what the effect will be if a duty of immediate performance is breached."[199] Duties are inferred mostly by the promises of the contract.[200]

Remedies -- Remedies are mostly apparent for breach of contract issues. As Miller Law outlines, there are a multiple of remedies for breach of contract, which include:

    1. Compensatory Damages

    2. Specific Performance

    3. Injunction

    4. Rescission

    5. Liquidated Damages

    6. Nominal Damages[201]

Remedies for breaches may be outlined in the contract or sued in court for after a breach. There is another two papers in this thesis on remedies and reparations.

Rights – As Rohwer et. al. outline: "contract rights are property rights and as with most property rights, there are strong policy reasons to make them transferable".[202] Once

---

[198] Rohwer et. al. <u>Contracts in a Nutshell</u>. 8 Nutshell Series (2017).
[199] <u>id.</u>
[200] <u>id.</u>
[201] Marc Newman. <u>6 Common Remedies for Breach of Contract</u>. Miller Law (2021).
[202] Rohwer et. al. <u>Contracts in a Nutshell</u>. 8 Nutshell Series (2017).

a duty has been fulfilled and likewise a contract: ownership of rights of property transfer.[203]

A good example of this is a home builder's materials are his until he contracts to build a house for a buyer, and thus, after the house is built, the rights of property to the materials that built the house are transferred from the builder to the owner. Simple process here.

Restitution -- Restitution is basically the idea of a party being made whole again, no matter what happened.

An example of restitution for a contract would be: some corporation bought a city park and made it a motel (that was later run-down) and after years of fight, the city decided to implement restitution and tear down the run-down motel in order to make a new park. This is a common example of a city-contract version of restitution.[11]

MODIFICATIONS, BENEFICIARIES, & BENEVOLENCE

Of course, follow-up definitions in this section:

Modifications – Simply put (by Up Counsel):

---

[203] id.

A modification of contract is any change, in part or whole, occurring to a legally binding agreement between two or more parties. Any contract can be modified before or after signing the agreement, but all parties must agree to the changes. If any party doesn't agree to the modification, the changes are invalid.[204]

Beneficiaries – The two main beneficiaries of most contracts are the buyer and the seller. However, "contracts may be formed in which one party's performance is to be rendered directly to a third party or the performance will indirectly confer a benefit upon a third party".[205] In that case, "a third party acquires the right to enforce a contract only if the court finds that the principal parties to the contract intended to create legally enforceable rights in the third party."[206]

A small but useful note in contract law.

Benevolence – Shortly here: there is a benevolence element to many contracts. Tipping is a great example. COVID-19 tipping made the standard 20%+, but this is a courtesy of the buyer, which means the ending result involves some sort of benevolence or appreciation for the good or service. This is mostly for services rather than goods, though, often, there is crossover and buyers provide benevolence-type-funds for goods.[207]

---

[204] Up Counsel Staff. Modification of Contract. Up Counsel (2021).
[205] Rohwer et. al. Contracts in a Nutshell. 8 Nutshell Series (2017).
[206] id.

Another good example is discounts for being a regular. No explanation needed here, save the supplier is now providing the benevolence.

DUTIES & DISCHARGE

Duties -- Contractual duties or obligations are basically the things required to fulfill the promises of the contract. In other words, contractual duties are:

> Those duties that each party is legally responsible for in a contract agreement. In a contract, each party exchanges something of value, whether it be a product, services, money, etc. On both sides of the agreement, each party has various obligations in connected with this exchange.[208]

Discharge – Discharge is the termination of the contract: though it can arise from quite a few things. The first (and easy one) discharge is performance: i.e., the job was done.

Other discharges include release (often for a fee), rescission (a cancellation), substitute contract or alternate agreement, novation (a newcomer comes in to take over), account stated (basically just a bill issued), and partial payments/work, etc.[209]

---

[207] Info from general knowledge of being a consumer.
[208] Legal Match Staff. Contract Obligations. Legal Match (2018).
[209] Rohwer et. al. Contracts in a Nutshell. 8 Nutshell Series (2017).

ADDENDUMS, AMENDMENTS, & ALTERNATIVE DISPUTE RESOLUTION

Finally, the last section of definitions (these from a contract drafting book); here we go:

Addendums – Addendums are new terms added to an agreement and must be signed/agreed upon by both parties. They are basically the same as amendments, though amendments change language already in the agreement while addendums are purely new.[210]

Addendums are commonly used in contracts to 1) establish new prices, 2) add a new product or service, 3) add a new territory or other license enhancement, 4) run a special joint program, and 5) impose a new restriction and 6) add other changes.[211]

Amendments – Amendments make changes or add new terms to a contract and also need to be signed off by both parties.[212]

Amendments are used in a similar fashion to addendums.

Alternative Dispute Resolution – Contract negotiations can be tough. Things like mediation can improve the handling of contracts and disputes between parties; breaches and other contractual breakdowns and issues may arise and thus make

---

[210] Paul Swegle. Contract Drafting & Negotiation for Entrepreneurs & Business Professionals. Business Law Seminar Group (2018).
[211] id.
[212] id.

alternative dispute resolution highly important, oftentimes, in terms of contracts.[213]

WHY CONTRACTS CAN BE PROBLEMATIZED

OK back to some prose. Contracts can be problematized for a million and one reasons. We've touched upon abusive, unfair, "obligating," and other various types of bad contracts in terms of definitions. I think imagining unfair contracts can be easy and should be recognized as something that is a problem with the law. The minimum wage contracts offered to workers is a prime example, and there are a myriad of other examples where people are exploited by contracts. Whether it's a business unfairly working or discriminating against employees, bad contracts that are illegal among differing people (abusive here even if not a valid contract due to legality issues), and other issues of the like.

Another other thing is, if you're not a lawyer: you're not necessarily going to be truly equipped to write or even fully understand contracts.[214] Writing contracts and contract interpretation is tough, especially with specialized industries. The layperson is easily lost on the issue of such.

My big question though is, why are there not more solid remedies for contracts save breach of contract? And even that seems to protect the contract writer more so than the signer (often the vulnerable one), which seems unfair.

Perhaps remedies like "unwarranted contract," "unfair conditions," and "declaratory review" could all help the struggle of people being bound by unfair contracts. It

---

[213] id.
[214] id.

seems as though the law should have more remedies against bad and unfair contracts. But, alas, here we are.

My mentor, who edited this paper, suggested that entire papers could be written about alternatives to breach of contract in terms of contract law... I agree, and I think you could somehow modify contracts to somehow expressedly include provisions like "needing to be simple for the public" or "contracts not being valid unless fair." These simple changes or others could be a gamechanger for people in terms of the contracts they sign.

THE CONTRACTS WE SIGN DAILY

We sign nonsensical contracts (or agreements) daily. From PayPal to Venmo, Amazon, Hulu, and Disney; stores we frequent; debit and credit cards we use; websites we virtually travel to, etc.

We may not have even been a) aware, b) caring, c) fully or even somewhat reading or, most importantly, d) really in agreement with these contracts we've signed. It's bullshit and everyone knows it; whether or not these opt-in rules are truly binding is a certain question/problem of the law.

The fact that we, as a society, are coerced into these agreements to continue capitalism/modernity and yet, we as people, have no idea what we are truly signing is an issue.

This is certainly a problem of the law.

CONCLUSION: "THIS IS WHY PEOPLE FANTASIZE ABOUT CONTRACTS WITH THE DEVIL; PEOPLE WILD"

The complication in contracts is why people are so intimidated by them and are fascinated/overwhelmed/etc. by them.

The mere fact that contracts are simply an agreement but can be as complex as an entire course/profession/books/etc. is amazing and could very well be a problem of the law.

The law is supposed to be at least somewhat approachable: this paper shows that contracts are indeed not despite their simple nature. Again, this is perhaps an issue the law should look into correcting.

_____

"I'm not apologetic, if you don't like it, it's probably 'cause you don't get it

And you can tell the world that you heard I said it

And I ain't talking about me, I'm talking 'bout the ones who represent what I believe

The fresh kids, the what comes next kids; The see you at the art exhibit, oh, hell yes kid

The politic kids, the be your thing and declare your independence kids

If I'm a vote for something, I'm a go Barack the vote this year

I'm talking 'bout the ones who said enough; The I got too much I don't give a what in my cup

The I don't care what the next man is sayingI'm just saying to the industry, this is fuck you, signed sincerely

Oh, yeah; Oh, here we go again; People talking shit but I don't give a damn

Everything I'm not makes me everything I am

Ooh, ooh, ooh, yeah; Oh, here we go again

People talking shit with no pot to piss in

But everything I'm not is everything I can; I can do anything

I remember the Doc saying, "What you gon' do? Girl, you 17"

(Ooh, ooh, ooh, ooh); (Ooh, ooh, ooh, ooh)

'Ye ripped on this track, made it into a jam

I just borrowed it just to tell you who I am"

-- Solange

"The 'Settlement' Problem"

TABLE OF CONTENTS

INTRODUCTION: "THE SETTLEMENT ISSUE IS A HUGE ONE"

THE CIVIL SETTLEMENT EXAMPLE

THE CORPORATE SETTLEMENT EXAMPLE

THE CRIMINAL SETTLEMENT EXAMPLE

CONCLUSION: "POWER BALANCES ARE CRUCIAL TO UNDERSTAND IN THE ISSUE OF SETTLEMENTS"

> "Say he rappin' and he trappin'
> But he really undercover"
> -- Rich the Kid

INTRODUCTION: "THE SETTLEMENT ISSUE IS A HUGE ONE"

Settlements in civil, corporate, and criminal cases happen significantly more than trials given the numbers-- 80%-92% of civil disputes are settled, for example--though are a complex and troubled issue (as is much the law, to be honest) concerning advantages and disadvantages to defendants (namely), judicial systems, prosecutors, public defenders, lawyers in general, and the general society. So, they are important for many reasons and can/should be analyzed in many ways.[215]

There are many reasons for the existence of massive amounts of settlements but also many reasons as to why settlements can be problematic.

This paper discusses the issues of settlements in civil, corporate, and criminal senses; and concludes with a discussion of the importance of power balances in settlements.

THE CIVIL SETTLEMENT EXAMPLE

In terms of civil cases, why is it good to settle? Well, settling:

> 1) Relieves you from an actual trial, which could be expensive, time-consuming, and lengthy.[216]
>
> 2) Does not put you in the high percentage of people wo are wrong about their claim that go to trial (56%-66% of people think they have a bigger claim than they actually do)[217]
>
> 3) Allows for settlement funds or other perks from settling[218]
>
> 4) Enlists game mentality which is often beneficial for negotiation of settlement terms[219]

---

[215] Jonathan Glater. <u>Study Finds Settling is Better than Going to Trial</u>. New York Times (2008).
[216] <u>id.</u>
[217] <u>id.</u>
[218] <u>id.</u>

5) Makes the system more efficient (less people in court) with people settling civil cases[220]

All good things. Though, one might not settle because of:

1) The rare case that expected returns (in various ways) of trial greater than settlement numbers[221]

2) The opposing counsel is giving you a bad deal in terms of the settlement[222]

3) Other reasons pertaining to trial being a better option than settlement (such as revenge, trial significance, or other "more rare" issues)[223]

Civil settlements can often go well given the perks of settlement (settlement money, no trial, more peaceful process, etc.), though the next two sections are a bit more debatable as to whether or not settlements are truly a "net beneficial" phenomenon for the law community and society in general.

THE CORPORATE SETTLEMENT EXAMPLE

Corporate settlements are a trip, namely due to forced mediation/arbitration. You simply can't sue many of the top corporations you may associate with due to the clauses in their terms and conditions of using their products or services.[224] Stolen images, privacy issues, property

---

[219] id.
[220] id.
[221] id.
[222] id.
[223] id.
[224] Megan Leonhardt. Consumers Can't Sue Some of the Biggest Companies in the US. CNBC (2019).

issues, all come up from this[225]. Arbitration with corporate companies is biased due to:

    1) The company's favor (home-cooking)

    2) Cheaper and faster

    3) Final decisions

    4) Fairing better than trial (?) (think of all the powerful lawyers that corporations have)

    5) Biased & secretive process[226]

Basically, it's a rigged system.[227] Here are some of the challenges facing someone in the process of arbitration with a corporation:

    1) Need for ample documentation of issue and solid proof of a claim

    2) Settlement consideration v. a tough corporate defense team

    3) Possibilities of the corporation appealing a less than optimal decision

    4) Long trials and the chance of losing the trial[228]

    Though, there are times where corporations do get disputes that require massive payouts:

    1) BP Oil Spill ($20B Payout)

    2) Bank of America Housing Market Scandal ($16B Payout)

---

[225] id.
[226] id.
[227] id.
[228] McMath Law. What Are the Challenges of Suing a Major Corporation. McMath Law (2019).

3) Enron Accounting Fraud ($7.2B Payout)

4) USDA Racial Discrimination ($2.3B Payout)[229]

Another example of a new-age version of this is the push to sue corporations for climate change, which is a definite part of the future of litigation[230]. This is based on a "scientific, discursive, and constitutional context."[231]

Yet another example is civil rights suits, which corporations have paid out to the tune of $2.7B since 2000.[232] "Hushed, sealed, and silenced victims" highlight a culture of racial, sexual, and other discrimination needing to be addressed in corporate law.[233] Violations and penalties for greed, cheating, and the dirty side of a race to the top all come to the light in this topic.

Finally, corporate bribery is a final issue/example given in this civil suit section. Corporate crime is a certain issue in the US today and allegations and enforcements are "bundled" (many cases in one decision) which often allows companies to: efficiently settle cases; have smaller bills for a plethora of violations; and it also incentivizes multilateral enforcement, which is good for the corporations.[234]

THE CRIMINAL SETTLEMENT EXAMPLE

---

[229] Cheapism Staff. 27 of the Biggest Lawsuit Settlements Against Corporations. Cheapism (2020).

[230] Ganguly et. al. If at First You Don't Succeed: Suing Corporations for Climate Change. The Nation (2018).

[231] id.

[232] Michelle Chen. Corporations Have Paid Out at Least $2.7 Billion in Civil-Rights and Labor Lawsuits Since 2000. The Nation (2018).

[233] id.

[234] B. Hock. Policing Corporate Bribery: Negotiated Settlements and Bundling. Policing & Society (2020). Multilateral enforcement is a process where corporations can bundle cases and settle in big settlements as opposed to deal with any one case individually.

Criminal settlements are certainly the worst example of justice in terms of the three examples of settlement groups we've discussed (though corporate settlements are pretty damn bad too).

There are many issues with corporate settlement that include:

1) Prosecutors making trial a tough option for defendants with their plethora of too[235]

2) Leverage for prosecutors in plea deals leads to bad deals for defendants[236]

3) Civil settlements related to criminal cases can be seen as an admission of guilt or evidence[237]

4) Offering the "whole truth" in a plea deal can lead to violence and other in communities when people "snitch"[238]

5) Prosecutors can be very coercive and, again, often give bad deals due to leverage[i]

6) Issue of false convictions or taken plea deals (usually due to fear of harsh time)[239]

7) Coverups of prosecutor misconduct[240]

8) Issue of the status quo of the system of the "New Jim Crow"[241]

---

[235] Russell Gold. Civilizing Criminal Settlements. Boston University Law Review (2017).
[236] id
[237] Daniel Blinka. 7 Wis. Prac., Wis. Evidence § 408.2 (4th ed.). Wisconsin Practice Series TM (2021).
[238] Markus & Dickinson. § 30:10. Plea, offer to plea, or related statement. Ohio Trial Practice (2021)
[239] id.
[240] id.
[241] id.

All big issues.

Though, the advantages to plea bargains are:

1) Lighter sentences

2) Reduced charges

3) Case being over[242]

And still yet, the downsides are:

1) Prosecution could have little to no case and offer plea deal as a cop-out

2) The chance of being found "not guilty" at trial

3) Coercion possibility

4) The prosecutor offers a non-binding agreement unless the court confirms the deal

5) The potential criminal record that comes with accepting a plea[243]

All good tidbits to know about the issue of settlements in a criminal sense.

CONCLUSION: "POWER BALANCES ARE CRUCIAL TO UNDERSTAND IN THE ISSUE OF SETTLEMENTS"

There are economic models as to the cost of plea bargaining and deals.[244] A literal scientific system of equations to this shit that destroys lives (due to lives lost

---

[242] HG Staff. What Are the Advantages and Disadvantages of Accepting a Plea Bargain. HG.org (2021).
[243] id.
[244] Sanford Weisburst. Judicial Review of Settlements and Consent Decrees. University of Chicago Legal Studies Journal (1999).

behind bars), corporate domination, unfair dealings by powerful players, and such of the like.[245]

The power imbalances (rich-poor, prosecutor-defense, corporation-individual) are a critical study in terms of understanding settlements.

What are the civil power imbalances in settlements?

What are the corporate power imbalances?

What are the criminality power imbalances?

What are the other power imbalances in settlements?

"Never been your average girl; So take time with me, take time

Baby talk to me with some action,; Think I got a place for your passion; Cool down, simmer"

-- Mahalia

"The 'Planning' Problem"

TABLE OF CONTENTS

INTRODUCTION: "MY STORY OF "TRUSTS & ESTATES" CLASS

IT WAS FUNNY THOUGH, THE PROFESSOR WAS COOL ABOUT IT

---

[245] id.

THE POINT BEING: WILLS, TRUSTS, & ESTATES ARE NO JOKE

MORBID, BUT FULL OF FASCINATING STORIES

CONCLUSION: "THE LAW CAN TRULY BE FASCINATING, BUT..."

> "I can't breathe (Chopsquad), I can't breathe, 999
> Waiting for the exhale
> I toss my pain with my wishes in a wishing well
>
> I can't breathe, I'm waiting for the exhale
> Toss my pain with my wishes in a wishing well
> Still no luck, but oh, well
> I still try even though I know I'm gon' fail
> Stress on my shoulders like a anvil
> Perky got me itching like a anthill
> Drugs killing me softly, Lauryn Hill
> Sometimes I don't know how to feel"
>
> -- Juice WRLD

INTRODUCTION: "MY STORY OF "TRUSTS & ESTATES" CLASS

I was enrolled in Trusts & Estates at DU Sturm College of Law during my final semester (Fall 2021) for 6 weeks until I dropped it. The class was a popular and necessary class for 3L's, and I was lost from the get-go, much like I was in Legal Profession.

Though, as a caveat, I was studying with a packed 6-day-a-week, 16-unit course load, of which only 12 units were necessary for my graduation. I wanted to learn Trusts & Estates generally, though this course called for a deep study I was unwilling and unable (with my other courses and thesis) to pursue.

Anyhow, I learned the following general things about the study of trusts and estates:

- The study is hard and a lot to understand
- The study is dramatic and calling for a tough wit
- The study is complex and nuanced
- The study is also morbid and sad
- As it is disappointing and depressing at times
- It can be satisfying at times, though
- The study is specific and field-driven

Personally, I thought to myself, wills are:

- Much more than expected
- Fascinating, morbid, and lots could go wrong
- Definitely a specialized subject within the realms of the law

IT WAS FUNNY THOUGH, THE PROFESSOR WAS COOL ABOUT IT

Like I said, I quit the course, but the professor understood and was chill about it. The course is meant to be a tough and rigorous study, not a primer.

THE POINT BEING: WILLS, TRUSTS, & ESTATES ARE NO JOKE

Wills and trusts, and the running of estates (of the deceased at least) is a deep and complex study, and I constantly, while in this course, wondered if wills should be more simplified so as to not have a complex and often seemingly, deeply nuanced system of law.

I get it, you may have a lot of money at the end of life and things are complex. But the level of depth to wills makes me think that we could somehow simplify this.

_____
_____

Is the complexity of wills a problem of the law (or society in general)?

MORBID, BUT FULL OF FASCINATING STORIES

I will say though, the wishes of the dead and their needing to be carried out by the living, and all things related to this field: are genuinely fascinating, and I enjoyed learning the stories of cases within the field. But geez, man, does the field need to be as complex as it is?

CONCLUSION: "THE LAW CAN TRULY BE FASCINATING, BUT..."

Is the law often if not at least sometimes much more complex than need be?

"Stuck in emotions,

And I don't know what they mean..."

-- LEON

"The 'School Diversity' Problem"

TABLE OF CONTENTS

THE PROBLEM THAT IS THE COLLEGE & UNIVERSITY SYSTEM

THE DIVERSITY IN COLLEGES & UNIVERSITIES ISSUE

 THE SCHOOL TO PRISON PIPELINE FOR MINORITY, URBAN, & POOR YOUTH

 THE ISSUE OF NON-DIVERSITY AT COLLEGE

 THE CAMPUS STAFF, SODEXO WORKERS, ETC. ISSUE & HOW IT   RELATES TO DIVERSITY

 THE FRAT/SOROR, STUDENT GOV., SPORTS, & CLUBS ISSUE & DIVERSITY

 THE PROFESSOR-IDEOLOGY AND PROFESSOR-LOYALTY ISSUE & DIVERSITY

 THE STUDENT FREEDOM & STUDENT DISCIPLINE ISSUE & DIVERSITY

 OTHER PRESSING UNIVERSITY ISSUES THAT CONCERN DIVERSITY

CONCLUSION: "DIVERSITY MATTERS AT SCHOOL: IN MOST ALL FACETS"

"Faces could tell will I push on
But it's the approach, that helps it on

Lost in your sayin' and in your charm
But I should be warned before I fall

Baby, I'll go out of my way, you know that
Maybe, you should do the same out of respect
Baby, I'll go out of my way, you know that
Maybe, you should do the same out of respect"

-- RIMON

THE PROBLEM THAT IS THE COLLEGE & UNIVERSITY SYSTEM

I've studied higher ed in a lot a "fashions":

- My mom was a high school counselor and I've always loved reading/writing
- I have an M.Ed. in Higher Ed Leadership & Policy and a BA in Cultural Studies

- I've attended Tulane University, the University of La Verne, EdX, the University of Southern California, UCLA Extension, HarvardX, the University of Washington, and the University of Denver (8 collegiate programs)
- I am (still) studying College Counseling at UCLA Extension despite HarvardX, UW, and DU graduate programs making it exceedingly tough (I have graduated from all the latter ones though)
- I wrote an M.Ed. thesis on marginalization in education and this MLS thesis on social and corporate legal issues.

So, yeah, I've got a background in higher ed.

The book, *Fundamentals of College Counseling*, greatly explains the landscape of the collegiate system and how it is riddled with culture, issues, loyalties, stances, and all the like. It's so interesting to be on the "opposite" side of college, as a non-undergraduate, though still in it as a "seasoned vet" 2nd (or 3rd year, if you will) graduate student. I know the college system, but every year countless students are befuddled with it.[1]

Training students for college is thus a big issue and one that is also riddled with culture, issues, loyalties, stances, and the like ☐.[2]

These issues are often difficult because of culture and social interactions of large (and small) groups of people with often adversarial views (such as a lawsuit).

You may see why understanding the law and higher education studies are great for me! But lawyering and being a higher ed professional; yeah, I'll probably pass!

Aside from what I experience now, I know that in college and grad school I've transferred, moved around, etc. and never quite found a diversity that truly made me proud, etc.

Tulane was mostly white (which was a lot); ULV was decently diverse but mostly white and LatinX and I felt like I didn't fit; EdX and HarvardX were fully online and not time bound, so community was nonexistent; USC was diverse but in LA everyone has their own gig they're driving on, community is scarce; UW was mostly white and Asian and again I stuck out; and DU....... preppy Denver (mostly white, but decently diverse) -- where was I supposed to fit in as a culturalist?

This paper is centered by Critical Race Theory, but branches out to queer theory, feminism, disability theory, immigrant theory, and the like.

The main questions I have (for this work) are centered around the question of diversity (ethics) on college campuses, and whether or not the law can enforce diversity efforts further?

THE DIVERSITY IN COLLEGES & UNIVERSITIES ISSUE

Diversity, at many colleges (elite, middle-tier, etc.), is an issue. Whether it's an elite Ivy or a community college, often diversity is left wanting at many institutions. Though, we know that diversity is superbly important for development and engagement, key markers of retention in college. This deficit is problematic for diverse students and the ecology of colleges as a whole.

Student development is arguably the main thing colleges and universities do. This is not very debatable. Though, the discussion of how students develop is diverse, as is the discussion of implementations from the university. Inputs and outputs if you will. How students develop may be socially, ethnically, sexually, through a gender lens, through ability, through competence, and all the like. Development is certainly not a monolith.[3]

So, if student development is central to colleges and U's, so then too has to be engagement. Engagement measures a student's interests and the time spent doing them. Without engagement, students risk not matriculating through the grades and ultimately making it through college. Engagement, well the right balance of such, is key for student development and thus to colleges in general. Engagement is already pillared by diversity in both activity, activity type, and activity offerings.[4]

Diversity (being central in both student development and student engagement) in activity offerings, people, professors, staff, and the like is thus central to what colleges and universities do, as without it, students may not be a) engaged or b) be able to develop.

My first major question is then: can diversity be legally required somehow?

If you made it a 14th Amendment discussion, one would certainly have an opportunity for such. Equal opportunity and protection under the law could certainly be triggered by a lack of diversity found on a college campus.[5] **Whether it's the lack of accessibility for a disabled person, perhaps a racial issue for a minority**

student, a gender issue for trans students, or some other form of a school being discriminatory on the grounds of equality could certainly find colleges and universities in hot water with the law. It makes complete sense as well, given that diversity in development and engagement are central to the mission of higher education institutions.[6]

There are a few quintessential items that the Education and the Law text for the course I wrote this paper for describes, which include:

- **The broad agreement in the legal field that you have a right to your education via the 1st, 4th, and 14th Amendments of the U.S. Constitution**
- **That the Brown v. Board Decision of 1954 allows for a right to equal opportunity and equal protection in terms of an education**
- **That generally the law has a duty to uphold equal opportunity of education and protection against discrimination in education**
- That schools are "at the service of students, not the other way around"
- That there are startling achievement gaps in America based on racial, gender, and other lines
- **That a lack of diversity could call into question education quality and educational quality measures/policies/initiatives**
- **That helping diverse students is ultimately an equal opportunity, equality-driven, and quality issue for all schools**[7]

All very clear either directly restated or directly inferred from this text.

Ultimately, diversity is an equal opportunity issue at its heart, which is indeed and very much protected by the 14th Amendment. Again, this is very clear.

Is diversity in colleges and universities a legal issue in terms of educational quality, educational fairness, and equal opportunity?

THE SCHOOL TO PRISON PIPELINE FOR MINORITY, URBAN, & POOR YOUTH

So why can't schools just fill their ranks with more queer, disabled, queer, and people of color? Well... that's a long story I'm somewhat unwilling to draw out and tell.

However, I will say that the marginalized face many issues starting with the school to prison pipeline, but also tons of troubles in the pursuit of things like a) an education, b) a job, and c) a productive lifestyle.

This section draws on three key works: *Career Choices, The New Jim Crow,* and *Reconnecting Disadvantaged Young Men.* We start this with an exercise. Imagine a black, brown, queer, disabled marginalized youth asking themselves the following questions from a very simple and straightforward Career Choices book, and how those questions might be problematized by a marginalized experiences (adverse experiences, record, outlook, etc.). Here we go:

Who am I? How do I define success? What are my passions, values, traits?

What do I want? What are my ideals? How can I make them attainable?

How do I get there? How do I stay there? How can I not be detoured?

What is my attitude about all this? Where do I go to start or continue?[8]

That could be a really emotional gathering for them (and maybe for you thinking about it too).   This is a basic level of "future consideration," but for someone affected by the school-to-prison-pipeline, this could be either life-changing, life-realizing, or life-daunting.

The New Jim Crow, as many know by now, is a work that describes (from the book's website):

> A stunning account of the rebirth of a caste-like system in the United States, one that has resulted in millions of African Americans locked behind bars and then relegated to a permanent second-class status—denied the very rights supposedly won in the Civil Rights Movement. Since its publication in 2010, the book has appeared on the *New York Times* bestseller list for more than a year; been dubbed the "secular bible of a new social movement" by numerous commentators, including Cornel West; and has led to consciousness-raising efforts in universities, churches, community centers, re-entry centers, and prisons nationwide. *The New Jim Crow* tells a truth our nation has been reluctant to face.
>
> As the United States celebrates its "triumph over race" with the election of Barack Obama, the majority of black men in major urban areas are under correctional control or saddled with criminal records for life. Jim Crow laws were wiped off the books decades ago, but today an extraordinary percentage of the African American community is warehoused in prisons or trapped in a parallel social universe, denied basic civil and human rights—including the right to vote; the right to serve on juries; and the right to be free of legal discrimination in employment, housing, access to education and public benefits. Today, it is no longer socially permissible to use race explicitly as a justification for discrimination, exclusion, and social contempt. Yet as civil-rights-lawyer-turned-legal-scholar Michelle Alexander demonstrates, it is perfectly legal to discriminate against convicted criminals in nearly all the ways in which it was once legal to discriminate against African Americans. Once labeled a felon, even for a minor

drug crime, the old forms of discrimination are suddenly legal again. In her words, "we have not ended racial caste in America; we have merely redesigned it."

Alexander shows that, by targeting black men through the War on Drugs and decimating communities of color, the U.S. criminal justice system functions as a contemporary system of racial control, even as it formally adheres to the principle of colorblindness.[9]

A writer for ThoughtCo summarizes the new-age version of this detrimental phenomenon, stating:

> The school-to-prison pipeline is a process through which students are pushed out of schools and into prisons. In other words, it is a process of criminalizing youth that is carried out by disciplinary policies and practices within schools that put students into contact with law enforcement. Once they are put into contact with law enforcement for disciplinary reasons, many are then pushed out of the educational environment and into the juvenile and criminal justice systems.
>
> The key policies and practices that created and now maintain the school-to-prison pipeline include zero tolerance policies that mandate harsh punishments for both minor and major infractions, exclusion of students from schools through punitive suspensions and expulsions, and the presence of police on campus as school resource officers (SROs).[10]

This system endangers the lives of many, many black and browns boys throughout the country and is a needed precursor of understanding to delve into this deep discussion of race, etc., as it concerns higher education spaces.

Edelman et. al., in their work *Reconnecting Disadvantaged Young Men*, discuss the issues of men being raised in tough situations and the resultant issues. Whether this is a personal trouble for the, very often, brown and black men or a larger societal issue of families, the courts, and the general social services network is an intriguing venture of the work that seems to devolve into the issue of, "Well, what for these men? Aren't they people too?"[11]

This eerie question is one that needs to be addressed for entities such as colleges and universities if they are interested in true social justice efforts. Diversity is central in this.

The need for these men (and women) to be studied and understood, helped and valued, brough incentives and perks, and all-around good/beneficial treatment is one of the myriad of solutions we need to enlist in the name of diversity. This much about the solution is evident clearly.[12]

Discounting these disadvantaged groups of men (and women) was law (Jim Crow), so why can't we build them back up with such? It seems as though disadvantaged peoples have very often been historically (and to this day) wronged by the law, so shouldn't there be a remedy for these groups of people? Couldn't colleges and universities being "legally diverse" be a solid start?

> *Does the school-to-prison pipeline have massive legislation efforts*
>
> *to fight the issue—and if not—why? Would diversity efforts in colleges be included?*

All that being said, here is a simple analysis of how I feel/have consistently felt, even growing up decently well-to-do:

You ever been told, "Look left, look right, they won't be here at the end."?

Ever heard that? It's scary because they're looking at you too.

If my Sociological Deviance background doesn't fail me:

- About 25% of black males go to prison
- About 25% of black males go to college
- About 25% of black males go to the military
- The other 25% do other things[13]

I looked left looked right and made it to college. For that, I'll always feel blessed. I ain't have to shoot it out (ball or a gun), I ain't have to not drop the soap, etc., etc. I got to study. You'd be hard pressed to find a white kid with a mindset like that (I'd believe); but it's the story colleges may need in today's era.

Imagine that narrative as a schizophrenic person, a queer person, or:

A black, queer, genderqueer, schizophrenic male

The narrative is tough but benefits others in higher ed spaces. We need gritty minds advancing us, not just the privileged and/or coddled ones. Though, another question I had was:

Could this issue of racial inequity in terms of education even be solved legally?

THE ISSUE OF NON-DIVERSITY AT COLLEGE

Whether or not diversity can be solved by the legal system is certainly a valid question, but the non-solving of this issue is an important deficit and deterrence we should all be aware of as well. Culturally, going into the complex arenas of politics and the like we are in 2020 on, we should all worry at the lack of the training of diverse minds to solve these ever-more-diversifying problems. Diversity, inherently, is a simple must in these times. Remember, that queer, disabled, black and brown bodies are the source of so so so many cultural/revolutionary/space-breaking trends/social changes that we should certainly want them as a forefront in the educated classes, not shied away to things like college hopping and lack of graduation due to cultural strife.

This country has stripped marginalized populations so much, it must realize that education is indeed a significant, if not the great (read GOAT), equalizer. And we'll gladly take it whether it's on Uncle Sam's bargaining table or not. But alas, I again, will defer from solutions in this problem-driven inquiry work.

A reminder here that culture is immensely important, perhaps starting a young age (younger for some than others, and some seem to never grasp culture well) and continuing on through adolescence and the transition into emerging adulthood and adulthood itself. The college prep (14-18) and college (18-26) years are formative, influential, mind- and life-shaping. College is a big deal, and arguably socialization is an even more important prerequisite to life one takes than any of the formal course on a transcript. Colleges and educators know this. So, in this sense... where college is a leader into life, why wouldn't we (at least) strive for diversity in experiences, experience, and all the like? Seems suitable for a diverse world, right?

Yet, this paper seems novel to even think about. Collegiate diversity somehow being solved by the law. You could say affirmative action as a lens into it, but what if we realized diversity at all turns as somewhat of a compliance to an acknowledged law of diversity, based in the 14th Amendment right to an equal opportunity and protection.

Thumbing through a few cultural texts I've amassed as an educator (namely *Why Are All the Black Kids Sitting Together in the Cafeteria, Everything You Wanted to Know about Indians, but Were Too Afraid to Ask*, and *Yes! We Are Latinos)*, reminds me that the different cultures you find in the US (from black to Native to LatinX to disabled to women to queer to anything that makes humans, human) are very diverse and studying any one population group can always be complicated by further delves into intersectionality, different oppressive systems, experiences and the stories told of them, and yes, statistics too. Culture is a beast and should be regarded as such. People are people for a reason, and we thrive when we a) listen to one another and our world speaking to us b) learn from it.[14]

Could we legalize diversity in schools? Is this a novel concept in terms of a holistic approach rather than simply quotas for race?

What does "diversity" legalized look like? Hmm...

If we enlist the 14th Amendment right to equal protection of the laws, diversity in schools, could diversity legalized be a remedy for the lack thereof and actually stand a chance in court?

I was disappointed with the diversity at my first college, and I ended up college hopping throughout college and grad school (not "truly fitting in" anywhere despite attending a plethora of school options both "highly official" and "not as official" settings of school).

This is troublesome and problematic to me. College hopping is inevitable though if diverse options are not available and readily apparent. Sadly, high school seniors cannot decipher diversity (which is OK neither can I after all my background(s) entail),

This is an insane subject to think about. Diversity is, indeed, a tough topic.

Could diversity be better pressed, perhaps legally, to help students that experience the phenomenon of college hopping and general transgressions caused by a lack of diverse American colleges and U's?

THE CAMPUS STAFF, SODEXO WORKERS, ETC. ISSUE & HOW IT RELATES TO RACE & DIVERSITY

From what I've experienced (on various campuses throughout the states) with campus staff, school cafeteria staff, etc., their rank are often a showing of the inequities schools and societies have. One clear example is Sodexo, who, services food for many campuses (like Tulane and DU among many, many others) and yet doesn't pay well and has had some serious allegations of racism. Don't believe it, here's a report to a 2005 $80 million settlement Sodexo paid for discriminating against black workers (https://www.corpwatch.org/article/us-sodexho-settles-large-racial-bias-case).[15]

Diversity issues can very often be shaped by cultural campus issues such as the racial, sexual, gender, etc. makeup of the staff, workers, students, and the like and their treatment by higher-ups. I know that campuses would benefit from a) human-fair policies for all employees b) diversity in staff. Those are surefire bets for healthier college campuses (from my higher ed knowledge), and would be a big win in terms of collegiate diversity, equity, and inclusion.

Can staff be included in our diversity efforts driven along by this paper?

THE FRAT/SOROR, STUDENT GOV., SPORTS, & CLUBS ISSUE   & DIVERSITY

My mom and dad (members of a black sorority and black fraternity) were always adamant about telling me how black frats were formed in a response to white fraternities and sororities not allowing black members, and thus cultural frats creating their own ranks of frats that are competitive, if not, more impressive than the "white frats."[16]

The "counter-culture" nature of black frats is another example of how diversity can solve issues on a campus, and I think it's prime time to acknowledge the benefit of these efforts that include Historically Black Colleges and Universities (HBCU's), black fraternities, pushes for accommodations for disabled people, queer theory as a response to heteronormativity, and all faucets of culture that serve to highlight and then turn on their heads, injustices that plague our world.

Social identity development for college students is a key aspect of development, as stated. Certainly, clubs and the like that are monumental and can serve to be life-long, like fraternities and sororities, should be acknowledged as modes to express, influence, and champion diversity.[17]

For me, I found community in school in a diverse range. I found a different way to vibe and fit in based on my interests and the like at each school I stepped foot on. At Tulane I worked on Student Government out of what I saw was necessary (I also had my frat), and at ULV I was cool with my music friends which was fun despite the tough year, and USC I had queer friends mostly as I emerged into more of who I truly am today, at UW I had my cultural friends (my ride or dies who were all woke, another deep part of me), and at DU I had us outcasts (MLS group and some other misfits).

I've developed in each of these settings by finding community that was true to me, myself, and I. I'm a different guy so I needed to develop the different me stuff (all at different times). It makes me think that there are more sides (and cities/U's) in me, and I'd like to keep exploring that. A coffee shop manager told me while I was at DU: "see the cities now, you're young, no girlfriend/boyfriend, no kids, no obligations, now's the time to explore!". He was right.

Clubs are the college springboard to real life socializations, activities, groups, and callings: they should be provided as diverse for students. Whether the law should require that and what that looks like is surely a thought to be had.

Could clubs and the like help mitigate diversity issues, much like black (and cultural in general) sororities and fraternities have?

THE PROFESSOR-IDEOLOGY AND PROFESSOR-LOYALTY ISSUE & DIVERSITY

It is often well-joked that most departments on most college campuses are liberal people. Teaching in higher education seems to bring that, save perhaps a political scientist or economist or perhaps STEM major. This "well known fact" may seem unfair, but the tenets of professorship probably lean with more openness as opposed to traditionality.[18]

This is somewhat and meant to be obviously speculative, but it makes the point that perhaps there are political leanings, perhaps even a heavy liberal bias in higher education and in education in general.... and to be fair, we should have diversity in political thought as a tenet of diversity kept as well. Diversity acknowledges arguments even if not as well found, it requires that. Some historical events (the Holocaust, slavery, Native genocide) may not require diversity with condemnation or lack thereof of atrocities, but the discussion of history is much like speech, regulated though free. We have to find this balance as Americans, especially in these tough times.

Diversity includes diversity in political thought in addition to racial makeups, sexual makeups, ability makeups, sexuality makeups, and the like.

I often wonder about the political leanings of professors. Conservative professors seem very rare certainly (an issue for some). But, so are black professors, women professors, queer professors, trans professors, disabled professors and the like, which is likely an issue as well.

All the diversity numbers make you think about the state of the world and all its inter-happenings...

Are professor political leanings in a more liberal (or conservative, etc.) direction, at least on a college campus, beneficial or detrimental?

Though, is a predominantly and proudly liberal (or whatever) faculty a discrimination issue?

THE STUDENT FREEDOM & STUDENT DISCIPLINE ISSUE & DIVERSITY

The *Education and the Law* text for the course this paper was for discusses free speech in education and higher education as a controversial and difficult field where "the correct course of action is often unclear."[19] Though, the Constitution allows for free speech as a pinnacle of the rights offered to Americans, and students "do not shed their free speech rights at the schoolhouse door." That applies to campuses too, though certain types of speech (like hate speech, fighting words, obscenity, harassment, etc.) are restricted.[20] The fact that freedom of speech is a tenet of campus activity is important for students and their developments (thoughts, ideas, speech, etc. is all free).

If we acknowledge we have a free speech right on campus, there should be room for a) diverse speech and speakers, but also b) a turn toward an acknowledgement of the right to equal protection as well. Protecting minority speech and experience should be given the utmost respect in the states, no matter the turn of the coin. Protecting diversity could ultimately be seen as a free speech issue as well.

Is diversity in speech (and the respect thereof) required for true freedom of speech?

OTHER PRESSING UNIVERSITY ISSUES THAT CONCERN DIVERSITY

Other presses for diversity include:

- Alternative Methods & Curriculums of Education
- Diversity of Fields and Experiences Offered by Colleges
- Diversity in Funding and Funding Sources/Outlets for Students
- Diversity & Conservation of Spaces/Campuses/Nature
- Diversity & Acknowledgement of School Funding/Donors
- Diversity of Grading & Evaluation (Essays, Projects, Tests, etc.)[21]

Diversity in colleges and universities is certainly a diverse issue in of itself.

This is all, however, rooted in educational equity in opportunity, protection, and the like.

Is diversity a solvable issue? Especially a solvable issue of the law?

CONCLUSION: "DIVERSITY MATTERS AT SCHOOL: IN MOST ALL FACETS"

If for nothing other than the development and engagement of students, diversity is truly key. And diversity takes many forms, customs, occupations, roles, and settings. This is important to note. Could diversity be fought for on college campuses, legally? Probably, yes given the concept of equal protection under the law. What that would look like though remains unseen and a topic for a restorative justice paper. But alas, this is not a thesis on solutions but rather one of problems. Is diversity in higher education institutions a legal issue or merely a social/institutional one? I don't know, you tell me.

Could "true" diversity definitively ever "take and keep shape" at elite, middle-tier, etc. colleges and universities?

"I'm from the South, never need a handout,

'Fore I let my people starve, I'll take it outcha mouf!"

-- Megan Thee Stallion

"The 'Rights' Problem"

INTRODUCTION: "THIS IS FOR Y'ALL WILD ASSES"

RIGHTS YOU CERTAINLY DO HAVE

RIGHTS YOU MAY OR MAY NOT HAVE

RIGHTS YO ASS DON'T HAVE

CONCLUSION: "C'MON FAM"

"Don't play a sport, but I ball

Answer the phone when I call."

-- 21 Savage

INTRODUCTION: "THIS IS FOR Y'ALL WILD ASSES"

      I wrote this work for all the wild asses out there (the Karen's, the Chad's, the various people that don't know what rights they do and don't have and yet insist on them like they're barred lawyers... yes, all these wonderful, truly wonderful people ▯). If you don't know what I mean, here is a cultural update:

https://nypost.com/article/what-is-a-karen-meme-name-meaning-explained/

> As they state:
> "Karen" has become social-media shorthand meaning a middle-aged white woman — potentially with an asymmetric haircut a la Kate Gosselin, circa 2009 — who makes a big fuss, and is not-so-blissfully ignorant. Recently, a fake American Girl doll ad for "Karen" caught the eyes of Twitter: The doll mock-up is of a sweatsuit-wearing, gun-wielding shopper who "refuses to wear a mask in public places."

I also wrote this work for people that would like a general refresher on human and constitutional rights in America.

I tried to write this work as straightforwardly as possible, for various non-stated reasons, though I will say that brevity here was important for many reasons both indicative of my style and the greater culture(s) these speak to.

Therefore, here are the rights and non-rights y'all (wild) folks may or may not have...

RIGHTS YOU CERTAINLY DO HAVE

To Your Life: Yup, you have the right to live your own life. No real restrictions there, do you! ☐[246]

---

[246] Human Rights Act. Article 2. (The Constitution arguably also gives you a right to "life").

To Your Liberty: Your liberty and what you do is on you boo-boo. I can't deny this. Doin' you is doin' you in America, for many. Though, I'm sure things like socioeconomic status (SES) and color could hold you back (hence the story of many, many amendments).[247]

To The Pursuit of Happiness: Pursue happiness as you are able*[248]. I think many, many people can speak on whether or not this is indeed a true right.

To Expression: The right to what you say and how you express yourself is another thing that's pretty on you. Throw in some hate speech or a certain setting like an airplane or train, maybe not so much. Also, be your view of a certain kind: you might face censorship. But expression is still very much up to you here in the states.[249]

To Your Privacy: As much as possible in this greedy-corporate world, you do have a right to protect what privacy you have left.[250]

To Your Religion and its Practice: Religion and its practice are another right you truly do enjoy. Though, I am sure that Christianity is a lot easier to "practice" than other theologies, etc. Just another thought to think of with rights.[251]

---

[247] US Const. Amend. V & Amend. XIV
[248] You can pursue happiness all you want, but without the true ability to claim it, you may be lost forvever.
[249] US Const. Amend. I & Human Rights Act. Article 10.
[250] US Const. Amend. IV.
[251] US Const. Amend. I.

To Your Property: You have a right to your property, as they are viewed as an extension of self in many instances and by many accounts. Your stuff is your stuff (save with massive debts and divorce, etc.) and thus usually you have a right to it. The US (and world) would literally be chaos without this right.[252]

To Not Be Illegal Searched or Seized: Don't let the cops or anyone else search you or your shit without reasonable suspicion of a crime or a fuckin' warrant.[253] That's a basic right. You have the right to not be searched and to not have yo shit seized without a warrant. Fight this tooth and nail y'all.[254]

To Due Process: You have the right to a trial if suspected of a crime.[255] You have the right to a fair and speedy trial. You have the right to remain silent and plead the fifth in court. Keep these in your arsenal of known rights (yes, even you, Karen).[256]

To A Jury Trial: You have the right to a jury trial if you get caught up in a criminal case. That's a right that justifies many criminalities that weren't, but I digress... who the jury is, is a separate story (though, it's supposed to be your peers), but yeah... If you get caught up, you have the right to be judged by a jury.[257]

---

[252] US Const. Amend. V & Amend. XIV.
[253] US Const. Amend. IV.
[254] US Const. Amend. IV.
[255] US Const. Amend. VI
[256] US Const. Amend. V.

To Not Be Fined Excessively: Yeah, so like, if they say you owe the feds a million and you broke (not Wesley Snipes) dawg they playin' you and you have a right to not be fined like that. This is a crucial right because many people receive fines that are astronomical compared to their livelihoods so yeah, again, this is important to note. Excessive fines are literally against your rights: fight them![258]

To Other Rights the Constitution Doesn't Name: You have other rights... when they come up, they'll come up and there'll probably be amendments for it. Whether or not you have the right to *you, yourself, while everyone else does* wear a mask in a private business is probably not one of those rights though Karen! ☐[259]

To States' Rights as They Apply to You: Shit... The amount to which I've enjoyed my STATE right to smoke weed in California, Washington, and Colorado as a consenting adult; b****, I'm payin' mad taxes, but it's my right to enjoy (in a legal manner ☐). STATES' RIGHTS in YOUR STATE are totally your right if it applies to the people! Enjoy them! Bask in them! They're what make the states unique oftentimes (like drinking and driving in Louisiana--all you need's a drink top and a passable drunkness level ☐). That's states' rights.[260]

---

[257] US Const. Amend. VI.
[258] US Const. Amend. VIII.
[259] Statutes, acts, etc. can afford you more rights.
[260] US Const. Amend. X.

To Not Be Enslaved Save When Criminalized: The 13th Amendment removes the allowability of slavery, though if you are incriminated you can be enslaved to certain extents, which is a very contentious issue.[261] Here I would suggest watching the documentary *13th*.

To Citizenship: You have the right to citizenship if you're born in or naturalized into the states. Citizens pay taxes, vote, live "freely," the whole 9, it's cool shit. Citizenship is actually one of the major benefits of American rights. We are Americans, a unique global tag.[262]

To Not Be Discriminated Due to Color or Race or Sex or Age: Ugh, yes, to not be discriminated against for those 3 or 4 classes (but also including religion and a few other instances of classes). *Called "protected classes," (inserting a true legal suggestion here, which is rare for this thesis), these most certainly should be expanded in the future of these states. Diversity, equity, and inclusion demand it.* This is expanded upon in the non-rights section.[263]

Not Have a Tyrannical President (per-say); Well, this really isn't true. The President cannot serve more than 2, 4-year terms. They can be tyrannical in a sense of rule, but not rule-time, apparently, given the last however many years. This is sadly very important in 2021 going on 2024... which is indeed shocking.[264]

---

[261] US Const. Amend XIII
[262] US Const. Amend. XIV.
[263] US Const. Amend. XIV.
[264] US Const. Amend. XXII.

To Representation via Congress, the President, etc.: You have the right to be represented by and to have Congresspeople and Senators and a VP and a President, etc. You have that right here in America, no matter how awful they perform ☐ or how poorly they represent you ☐.[265]

To Vote: You certainly have the right to vote or not vote (unless you're a felon, in which case you cannot vote). Use your votes wisely.[266]

RIGHTS YOU MAY OR MAY NOT HAVE

To Not Be Discriminated Against Based on Sexual Orientation, Culture, Income Status, Etc.: So, again, none of these are "protected" classes, so suing for protection via the Constitution may not be as fruitful as one might think. States will differ, but in terms of the Constitution, suing on the grounds of discrimination due to the listed classes.... Good luck ☐. Being poor, trans, an immigrant, etc., is often not something that will win you a case in America.

To Abortion: As we've seen recently (August/September 2021) in Texas, abortion is a in a perpetual fight as to whether it is a constitutional right for women, transwomen, or anyone else.[267] States' rights, representation, and voting

---

[265] US Const. Amend. XIV.
[266] US Const. Amend. XV.
267 Roni Rabin. Answers to Questions About the Texas Abortion Law. New York Times (2021).

Ashley Lopez. Texas Abortion Law Harms Survivors of Rape and Incest, Activists Say. KHN, NPR (2021).

can all swing this topic greatly, as it has for quite some time in America. This topic is unfortunately not going to subside any time soon and a fight for the rights of women is to be kept on-guard. Texas is so recent but throws salt on an old wound much injured.

To Healthcare: Healthcare, especially of certain types and those that aren't referred, are not a right in America. One of the many, "should this be a right? In Europe, blah blah blah..." In America, healthcare is getting better off (as it is still a major issue) but is still very much not a right to you, especially if you don't have a) money b) a job or c) a disability.

To Food: You don't really have the right to food in America, as plentiful as shelves are. Food costs and unless you qualify for free lunch programs or Eletronic Benefits Transfer (EBT or "food stamps"), food and especially healthy food is not a right, which is sad given the fact that stores are always so stocked (in many, many states) and yet hunger and food-affordability is a sickening problem. Food deserts, and the like are explained here: https://www.verywellhealth.com/what-are-food-deserts-4165971.

[268], getting "free" food with the rest of you Americans sounds horrendous and dangerous to the point that I might get killed trying to grab a few items in Safeway. I will gladly opt for food to not be free and thus not really a right. Y'all are some animals when pressed or given the opportunity.

Roe v. Wade, 410 U.S. 113 (1973)

[268] Mike Vogel. NewsDay. The great toilet paper wars of 2020 (2020).

To Safety: Again, safety isn't really a right.... I mean everybody is out here life and libertying, so safety is not really the priority (there are the heavily armed police though!). Though, in this argument I'm literally speaking as a Pioneer (DU Pioneers) and all my degrees are in the West so.... F*** it, let it ride stateside, am I right??

To Not Be Held Back by Biases: Haha bias I'm sorry you expected to get through America with the right for people to not be biased against you. Hahahaha I'm sorry they say educate don't laugh but that's hilarious. As a black, genderqueer, queer, schizophrenic male......

To Job Security: You don't really have a right to yo' job. You don't. Not really in any sense at any time. People get fired, businesses get shut down, things go wrong or weren't yours to truly have without discord in the first place. Yo' job is not a right. For many reasons not explained, but basically because you may not know your rights, or work "at-will," and the fact that many jobs are employer-slanted in terms of "rights," good luck trying to find actual job security save perhaps if you have a salary and that's built into your job.[269] You most usually (save like tenured professors and perhaps mega business owners) do not have a right to yo' job. Act accordingly or not I don't really care

---

[269] Personal experiences working (shitty) jobs.

Allison Green. No One Knows Their Legal Rights at Work. Slate (2020).

Liz Ryan. Ten Ways Employment at Will Is Bad for Business. Forbes (2016).

at this point. It's crazy to me how much employment drives America and yet there is still little job security.

To Employment at All: Again, you don't really have a right to any employment. You could be unemployed ya whole life if (un)able/confined to such. The bag is meant to be "got" in America, not just had.

To Not Be in Poverty: You don't really have the right to not be poor. I told you that and it's most definitely true. You have the right to pursue wealth if it's happiness's equivalent and you do so in a lawful manner, but you could also be broke your entire f******* life; the Constitution does not care. Nor will it really help. That's yo' job apparently.

To Be Allowed in A Store, etc.: You have the right to interstate travel and the right to go many, many places in America as a citizen. If people allow you on their private property even more is open to you. Be well, Americans and enjoy your range as free individuals. Though, remember, that many parts of the country feel uncomfortable to others based on their backgrounds and beings, which is an interesting twist on a "right."

To Be Allowed in A School, etc.: A lot, maybe most times, if you live there, you can probably go to school nearby (if in age limits, usually). Your kids can go to school where you live (save disciplinary or other issues of attendance), community colleges offer open enrollment, colleges across the nation (more than 2,000 in number) take applications from most anyone. If you're a citizen in America, school is usually something that you have a right to, or at least consideration or an opportunity for. Though, schools are not very equal and can shape lifetimes (often they do); getting a fair shake at school, as opposed to just "going" is a question of education and educational law not answered here (though is explored in the Education Law papers ☐).

To Be in A Workplace, etc.: You have the right to pursue work, but work *somewhere* certainly not. Felons and the underqualified know this well. Pursuing work is as simple as an application on the Internet or in person, but actually "working" and "continuing to work in/gain a check from" in a place of work is an entirely different story.

To Live Freely: *The "FREEDOM OF AMERICA" is in the eye of the beholder.* Many, many feel like they simply cannot go many places in these states or even be who they are to the fullest extent where they are or aspire to be. I am one of them, for many reasons namely blackness, queerness, and disability. Are you "truly and totally free" in America? Is anyone really? And if you are: that must be nice.

RIGHTS YO ASS DON'T HAVE

To Be in A Private Store or Otherwise and Not Follow Their Rules: So... private property is private and, save in the case of actual discrimination (again, remember the narrowness of classes, etc.), can allow or disallow WHOMEVER they want from their premises. So, yes, Karen, your ban at your local grocery store for the fact that you did not have a mask during COVID can disavow you from your shopping duties at their store as long as they'd like honey. You may not be allowed back in there and quite frankly if they banned you from the store, you have no right or business in their establishment honey, OK? Thank you.

To Verbally Abuse People in Threatening Ways: Threats, especially those unprovoked and not in self-defense, are not usually or at least always protected speech, so threatening or verbally abusing others in a threatening way is certainly not a right you have and could certainly land with a charge and a case.[270] Thank you.

To "Always Be Right" As the Customer or Privileged Person: Yeah, you may think you have this "right," but you're certainly not "always in the right" as the customer and again people can bar you from their business for most any reason that isn't discriminating.... Looking at y'all airplane/airport Karen's that are on the no fly-list.... (The airline and airport were indeed the "person" in the "right" ▢). You might be flying Spirit or not at all...

To Abuse the Law in A Substantial Way: Again, El Choppo went to jail. Tony Montana would've* went to jail. The people who killed Elijah McClain; R. Kelly; serial killers; campus shooters, you get where I'm going. The lawless and reckless go to jail; you simply do not have the right to abuse the law. The law is the law is the law. Minor infractions cause minor penalties, but substantial violations

---

[270] ALA Staff. Hate Speech and Hate Crime. American Library Association (2021).

are cause for disbarment from society as a whole, to be among people that have violated the social norms of society in the same or similar fashion that you have riddled the system.

Many Other Instances of the Abuse of Rights: The Constitution stating that you have other rights that aren't expressly admitted in the Constitution is a question that could truly change the world in a beneficial way (like the suggestion—a common suggestion—I've made of diversifying protected discrimination classes) or truly land you in some trouble (Karen ▫).[271]

CONCLUSION: "C'MON FAM"

Be wise with your rights... Otherwise, you could be in a whole heap of madness.

> "Keep a strap in the Jeep in case a bitch tweak
> Hope that nigga got some racks, 'cause this ain't cheap
> I'ma break the whole bank if he date me
> And hope I don't go in his pockets when he go to sleep"
>
> -- Renni Rucci

---

[271] Wiktor Osiatynski. Human Rights and Their Limits. Cambridge University Press (2009).

CORPORATE/ADMINISTRATIVE
20. Legislative Drafting – "The 'Legislature' Problem'"
21. Legal Profession – "The 'Client' Problem"
22. Corporations [Directed Research] – "The 'Corporate' Problem"
23. Administrative Law [Directed Research] – "The 'Bureaucracy' Problem"
24. Contracts [Directed Research] – "The 'Contractual Obligations' Problem"
25. Law Practice – The Law Firm as a Business – "The 'Law Firm' Problem"
26. Big Law – Practice of Large Firms – "The 'Big Law Firm' Problem"
27. Advanced Research for Legal Scholar – "The 'America' Problem

"The 'Legislature' Problem"

TABLE OF CONTENTS

INTRODUCTION

THE PROBLEM OF THE BILL PROCESS

THE PROBLEM OF THE SLOW PROCESS

THE PROBLEM OF CONTENTION AMONG PARTIES

THE PROBLEM OF NON-BEARED FUTURES

CONCLUSION: "THE LAW IS WILD"

"Get yours, cuz I'ma get mines today,

I ain't certain they won't put me in the ground today,

So I'm gone work like they gone put me in the ground today..."

-- August Alsina

INTRODUCTION

This paper evaluates the legislature as it relates to how the law is written (notably a limited scope of legislature here, not an expansive look into the problem that Congress is and various State Assemblies are).

THE PROBLEM OF THE BILL PROCESS

The process of a bill being passed is a bit complicated and can be very nuanced. Here is the basic (as in general) bill process:

1. Bill is requested (Sponsor to legislature) and drafted

2. Bill is docketed and brought up in Senate or Congress

3. Bill is assigned to a committee (most bills die here)

4. Bill is amended

5. Bill is either passed or doesn't pass in House or Senate

6. Bill is either passed or doesn't pass in other body

7. Bill is enacted (or not) and implemented/enforced (or not)[272]

Bills are needing to go through a stringent process to become law. Perhaps this is a problem. Perhaps Congress, being wealthy, white, and old is the problem. Of course, the process of the bill is tough and thus why most bills die in the process.

THE PROBLEM OF THE SLOW PROCESS

The bill process is slow and can drag on for months. When Congress or State Assemblies want to act they do, but that's rare and often controversial. If you want change with the government: you've got to be willing to wait. That's the nature of the bill and legislative process.[273]

THE PROBLEM OF CONTENTION AMONG PARTIES

Most Congress members are on two sides: Democrat and Republican (or liberal and conservative if you like). Party members usually vote along their block, so unless you have a majority in power, trying to pass bills can be tough. A one-party domination can mean tons of legislative efforts, sort of such we are seeing now under President Biden. This is an easy an important note: Dem's and Rep's differ. Is that a problem? Well, when it comes to the written law it certainly can be. The law differences between red and blue states can cause contentious legal issues of rights, torts, and all sorts of conundrums. The federal, state-v.-state issue adds to it. Contention among

---

[272] Referenced from Professor Whitlow's "Legislative Drafting" course at DU (2021).
[273] More ideas from Professor Whitlow's "Legislative Drafting" course. DU (2021).

parties is a real issue for the way the law is written and could certainly be considered a problem on a base and deeper levels.

THE PROBLEM OF NON-BEARED FUTURES

This section should be short, as it is a basic breakdown of two concepts involving the legislature and bills. Basically, the idea is two-fold:

> 1. The new year brings a new Senate/Assembly and they're not bound by the last year (in most cases). Basically, it's a clean slate. This means a lot in terms of elections, bills passed, etc. Is it something we should look into? Perhaps. It's a weird and somewhat confusing concept that the new Assemblies are not held by the old ones, in most cases, but certainly is something to consider when evaluating the written law.[274]

> 2. If your law, for whatever reason under the sun, can't be implemented, executed, enforced, etc. then it's not going to bear on people. The idea that, if once the bill is passed, a bill can't be enforced or truly implemented then it has no bearing other than being passed. Resolutions (bills meant for more honorary/symbolic purposes rather than actual laws) are often precisely fitting

---

[274][274] More ideas from Professor Whitlow's "Legislative Drafting" course. DU (2021).

of this criterion and are a prime example of bills with a non-beared future.[275]

Non-beared futures are an issue for bills and can be problematic on many levels.

CONCLUSION: "THE LAW IS WILD"

The law can be a whole lot, just like the federal government. Just something to consider.

"Homie needed help: I threw a alley-oop!"

-- Pacman da Gunman

"You a shoulda coulda; I'ma wisha a bitch would...
These bitches suwoop just like they should"

-- Bbyafricka

---

[275] Professor Whitlow. Id.

"The 'Corporate' Problem"

INTRODUCTION: SO WHAT? I'M A CORPORATE & SOCIAL LAW STUDENT; GET OVER IT AND YOURSELF

ARGUMENTS WITH FRIENDS OVER "CORPORATIONS"

CORPORATIONS IN GENERAL

    GENERAL ARGUMENTS FOR CORPORATIONS

    GENERAL ARGUMENTS AGAINST CORPORATIONS

A "CONSERVATIVE SOCIALIST" IDEOLOGY

CONCLUSION: BUSINESS IS THE HEARTBEAT OF AMERICA, JUST TO BE HONEST, BUT...

Fast, I'm coming in fast (uh-huh); First place, you coming in last (that's right)

I'm hitting that, hitting that gas; I'm hitting that, hitting that ass (my body)

I'm coming in fast (uh-huh); First place, you coming in last

I'm hitting that, hitting that gas; I'm hitting that, hitting that

Locomotion; We causing a commotion

I put it in, I put it in, I put it in motion; I put it in, I put it in, I put it in motion

Locomotion; We causing a commotion

Iciest bitch in the whole damn land; I hit the road in an all-white Lam'

I keep a fresh set up on my hands; You don't like me, but you on my 'Gram

How you look, how you look, how you sound, ho?; I'm a boss, I'm a brat, hard to handle

I'm a real life mood, a real life muse; Got some pretty-ass toes in my sandals

I can't help, I was born like this; Ain't my fault that you want my drip

Little bitter bitch could have been my friend; Now you gotta listen while I pop my shit"

-- Saweetie

INTRODUCTION: SO WHAT? I'M A CORPORATE & SOCIAL LAW STUDENT; GET OVER IT AND YOURSELF

Most people, when I tell them (which is rare) that I study corporate law in addition to socially driven law, they are often a) put off, b) wondering why I study corporations, and c) decently snarky about their disdain for corporations. Corporations are a toss-up to me though, and I think many, many people have the same sentiment towards these entities. So, I take it with a grain of salt when people are, a) b) and c), and often will add that I need to learn the corporate world if I want to change it. But I don't think corporations are all bad. I think they are simply needing to be bettered but a superbly valuable asset to the culture of the states.

So, so what I'm a corporate law student. Get over it.

ARGUMENTS WITH FRIENDS OVER "CORPORATIONS"

I've had a few frustrating conversations with friends about corporations. I think so many people are anti-corporation, but they use all types of products and services from corporations. What an oxymoronic issue.

Yes, corporations can be evil, manipulative, poorly run, abusive, and all the like, but to totally ignore all the good things corporations do is somewhat ignorant. The products and services afforded to us by corporations are so intriguing, and I think many people miss the point that while corporations are often pieces of work, they also are (collectively) way important to the continued brilliance of people in this country and world. As Mike Moffatt for Thought Co. outlines:

> Large companies can supply goods and services to a greater number of people, and they frequently operate more efficiently than small ones. In addition, they often can sell their products at lower prices because of the large volume and small costs per unit sold. They have an advantage in the marketplace because many consumers are attracted to well-known brand names, which they believe guarantee a certain level of quality.[276]

So, corporations really run the gambit of good and bad (just like us humans). One might want to think about the absolute powerhouse corporations are in order to break them down and see what the actual benefit of them is, or rather, critique them. My mentor mentioned that corporations came up with the COVID-19 vaccine, so they definitely do some type of good, at least some of the time.

CORPORATIONS IN GENERAL

Corporations are often bad and evil in many ways. Think about things like Amazon working their employees to death, Walmart not paying its workers a livable wage, the countless number of fast-food jobs that don't allow people to make enough to house and feed themselves[277], etc.[278] But companies also do a significant amount of good,

---

[276] Mike Moffatt. Corporations in the United States. Thought Co. (2020).
[277] Information from a general knowledge of companies with dangerous practices.
[278] There is also a plethora of articles that describe the evilness of corporations... Here are four of them:

which is hard to ignore. Amazon delivers much needed supplies to anyone in a matter of a few days (with a Prime subscription), Walmart allows people to shop for things at a massive discount, and we all love driving through fast-food places for our quick meals. There are certainly upsides and downsides to the nature of corporations.

As the Atlantic points out: "Large corporations are vilified in a way that obscures the innovation they spur and the steady jobs they produce."[279] The article continues on to point out many fascinating logical inferences about the way people feel about business (big and small) and the relative facts about corporations. One of the best points is that:

> In 2015, small enterprises were four times more likely to lay off their workers than large ones. Workers employed by large firms also earned more—on average, 54 percent more than workers at small companies. Companies with more than 500 employees offer 2.5 times more paid leave and insurance benefits and 3.9 times more in retirement benefits than workers at firms with fewer than 100 employees. Large firms are also more likely to be unionized, and they employ a greater share of women and minorities than small firms do, making Big Business an unlikely enemy of progressives.[280]

There are also, generally, good corporations out there. Hannah Durbin from the company *Classy* outlines nine in her article, and I touch on my favorite five[281]:

---

https://www.tampabay.com/news/business/corporate/from-bad-to-baddest-the-ten-nastiest-corporations-of-the-moment/2295964/
https://www.cracked.com/pictofacts-2171-evil-things-huge-companies-have-done
https://slate.com/technology/2020/01/evil-list-tech-companies-dangerous-amazon-facebook-google-palantir.html
https://www.thetoptens.com/most-evil-companies/

[279] Atkinson & Lind. Is Big Business Really that Bad? The Atlantic (2018).
[280] id.
[281] Hannah Durbin. 9 Socially Conscious Companies to Model This Year. Classy (2021).

Google

Google, in many opinions does well because of its environmental awareness, treatment of employees, and general contribution to the world. The company has been working on its carbon footprint (aiming to be carbon-free by 2030) and upping the awareness of other companies as it relates to their environmental impact. Finally, "[from] employee gift matching, to paid time off for volunteering, Google inspects nearly every part of their business with a social impact lens."[282]

Ben & Jerry's

As Durbin outlines:

> Ice cream tastes just a little sweeter when you know the makers work to promote safe, socially responsible ingredients and business practices. Since the 1980s, Ben & Jerry's has supported a number of important causes, many of which are directly tied to the business of making ice cream.[283]

Ben & Jerry's has fought against growth hormones used in cows, worked to encourage employees and others to better their communities, given social justice program grants, and fought against racism. "Ben & Jerry's impact is then further amplified by the Fairtrade social premium, an additional amount of money paid on top of the fair price that farmers receive."[284]

---

[282] id.
[283] id.
[284] id.

LEGO

LEGO is another company that is, at least, aiming toward some type of social awareness. Durbin details this saying:

> The LEGO Group is one of the most notable examples of how social responsibility can be an incredible asset to a well-known brand... In September of 2020, the LEGO Group announced that they were set to invest $400 million over the next three years to support their social responsibility and sustainability efforts... by the end of 2025, they are going to start by phasing out single use plastic bags and installing additional solar panels on all factories... By 2022, the LEGO Group is also aiming to reach eight million children around the world annually with learning through play. In collaboration with the LEGO Foundation, UNICEF, Save the Children, and local partners, the team is working to scale up programs that give children the opportunity to develop life-long skills.[285]

Warby Parker

Warby Parker is famous for their "We'll send you 5 pairs to pick from" business model. Though, their social justice model is another great thing about them, as they also provide glasses to those that are in need.[286] Durbin adds to this idea stating:

> Through their Buy-A-Pair, Give-A-Pair program, Warby Parker makes a monthly donation to their nonprofit partners, such as VisionSpring, to bring prescription eyewear to people in developing countries. The company has distributed more than eight million pairs of glasses since its start in 2010. As of April 1, 2020, a portion of purchases will

---

[285] id.
[286] id.

additionally go toward personal protective equipment and preventative health supplies for healthcare workers and communities in need.[287]

Microsoft

Microsoft is yet another shining example of a company dedicated to doing good in the world. Durbin outlines this saying:

> Microsoft changed the way the world works, studies, and plays with their computers and software. But their ambitions go far beyond the screen. The company... began its giving program in 1983 when the fledgling company raised $17,000 for charity. As their CSR web page explains, Microsoft's giving program has not only given time (employees in the U.S. volunteered more than 750,000 hours for nonprofits in 2020 alone), but also cash. In fiscal year 2020, the program raised over $221 million for nonprofits.

This list could have many more companies and many of them are indeed Top 9 or 10 material. Many companies do in fact do good for the world, though people certainly have a right to be skeptical.

Furthering the idea of corporate social responsibility, here is a link to the 2019 Aflac graphic (https://www.aflac.com/docs/about-aflac/csr-survey-assets/2019-aflac-csr-infographic-and-survey.pdf) that goes over many corporate social responsibility statistics and inferences that include:

- Purpose v. Profit
- Social/Business Impact
- Scrutiny & Forgiveness
- Generational Differences

---

[287] id.

- Expectations
- Bad Behavior
- Many Other Stats & Figures[288]

Businesses being "good" or "bad" is a tough debate. Though, given the research, perhaps corporations are not the worst thing in the world (though they could be bettered of course).

GENERAL ARGUMENTS FOR CORPORATIONS

"Advantages of a corporation include personal liability protection, business security and continuity, and easier access to capital."[289]

Other advantages include:

Competition: Businesses spur competition in the world and keep the world "a turnin.'" The American Dream is built on the ideas of manifest destiny and competition, and that's what businesses seem to do/provide. [290]

Global Stability: Put frankly: the world is better off as a whole with business deals spurring global conversations, innovations, and the like. Many companies are multinational and thus might have employees all over the world working toward a similar goal. This is, arguably, beneficial for the world.[291]

---

[288] Aflac. 2019 Corporate Social Responsibility Report. Aflac (2019)
[289] Skye Schooley. Pros and Cons of Forming a Corporation. Business News Daily (2020).
[290] Up Counsel. Corporate Personhood. Up Counsel (2021).
[291] id.

People-Backed Corporations: Behind the corporation and its ideals is almost always a person or group of people. Investors, directors, employees, and owners all benefit from, and are usually the backbone of the corporation.[292]

People are Protected: The limited liability of corporations makes it the company's problem, usually, rather than the direct employees or other members of the corporation. This is highly important for the sake of people being able to guide the business in a safe and sustainable manner.[293]

Inclusion in Society: People working for companies allows them to work, live, and thrive in terms of being in the world. Yes, there are lots of problems with this argument, but corporations clearly employ a ton of people worldwide and oftentimes enable them to live a better life than without a job.[294]

To add, *The Economist* writer K.N.C. gives these powerful things that would not exist without corporations:

> Without business we would not have:
>
> * Ships, trains, and cars
>
> * Electricity, lighting, and heating equipment
>
> * Most of our food supply
>
> * Most of our lifesaving pharmaceuticals
>
> * Clothes for our children
>
> * Our telephones and smartphones
>
> * The books we love to read

---

[292] id.
[293] id.
[294] id.

* The ability to access, more or less immediately, so much of the world's online information

And let's not forget your paycheck. "Meeting payroll," to invoke a now old-fashioned phrase, is nothing less than a heroic act.[295]

So, again, there are benefits to corporations.

GENERAL ARGUMENTS AGAINST CORPORATIONS

"Disadvantages of a corporation include it being time-consuming and subject to double taxation, as well as having rigid formalities and protocols to follow." (Business News Daily).

Other disadvantages include:

Businesses Being "Real": The weird conundrum that businesses are people, just not "natural" people is a distinction that is strange to many. The idea that a business is its own distinct person could easily be construed as disrespectful to actual people and in its most basic form: a lie for the sake of business.[296]

Lack of Morality: The lack of morality of corporations is often atrocious. This must be bettered in America in so many ways (pay, environmental-impact, treatment of employees, mental health time off).[297] My mentor sent me an article about a pregnant Amazon worker that lost her child duet to Amazon's condition. This is

---

[295] K.N.C. Why we should embrace big business. The Economist (2019).
[296] Up Counsel. Corporate Personhood. Up Counsel (2021).
[297] id.

terrible, but often the typical nature of tough-to-work-for companies.[298]

Corporate Personhood is Silly in Many Ways: The analysis of this by Up Counsel is kind of funny but very true. They say:

> A big part of personhood is feelings. Businesses have no feelings because they are not people. A business can't live. It can't die. Businesses do not feel love, get married, or have children. If a business is not alive, then it is not a person and does not deserve personhood.[299]

Businesses are Money-Driven: Businesses (save nonprofits and social entrepreneurships, etc.) usually have a main (but not only) goal of making money. Thus, most businesses are money-driven and money-first, which often creates a lot of problems, especially in terms of immorality.[300] Amazon is yet another good ("bad") example here.

Corruption of Big Business: Big business can yield a ton of corruption, unjust enrichment, abuse of power, and the like.[301] Also, money corrupts people, and corporations are a prime example of such.

Environmental Damage: Corporations are known to damage the environments they are in, that is no secret at all, and is the reason for the plethora of regulations in industries. *Future of Working*

---

[298] Lauren Gurley. Amazon Denied a Worker Pregnancy Accommodations. Then She Miscarried. VICE (2021).
[299] id.
[300] id.
[301] Future of Working. 19 Advantages and Disadvantages of Multinational Corporations. Future of Working (2021).

provides this analysis on how corporations can be especially damaging to developing countries:

> Most developing countries do not have the same level of regulation and oversight that the developed world maintains to protect the environment. When these firms decide to do business in the international market, they are subject to local laws – not the ones that govern their domestic headquarters – when working to obtain raw materials.[302]

Obviously, environmental damage is a factor here.

Overworked Employees: Many companies overwork their employees. Personally, I worked as a tutor for a company that wanted us working a minimum of 25 hours a week, which is a lot of students and a ton of unpaid prep time, while I was a full-time student. I tried and tried to communicate to them, but it was brutal because they kept adding and adding students to my already overworked load.

High Stress & Low-Paid Work Environments: Both high stress environments and low-pay are significant downsides to corporations, who often profits to the general wellbeing of their employees. Many, many companies fall under this reasoning flaw.

A "CONSERVATIVE SOCIALIST" IDEOLOGY

I believe in the institutions: law, education, business, culture, etc. I am skeptical of how things are often run, accomplished, dealt with, etc. oftentimes, which is why I study all these subjects to hopefully better them throughout the things I do in my life.

---

[302] id.

I also believe that the institutions are meant to serve the people. If an institution doesn't work for people or for the benefit of people, I'm pretty skeptical of it. Institutions are for the betterment of people in my mind.

I consider that to make me a conservative socialist, red and light blue. Say what you want about it, but I think I acknowledge both sides of all these arguments pretty damn well.

CONCLUSION: BUSINESS IS THE HEARTBEAT OF AMERICA, JUST TO BE HONEST, BUT...

Business is the heart of America and American capitalism. My mentor/professor included the President Calvin Coolidge quote which reads: "After all, the chief business of the American people is business. They are profoundly concerned with producing, buying, selling, investing and prospering in the world."[303] That's the analogy I love to think of: businesses here, there, and everywhere, that's the states I know. Small business, medium-size business, large corporations: all pumping much-needed blood to the people in this country. Nonprofits are also considered corporations, so, as my mentor mentioned to me, there is likely a company that does something you absolutely love/support for every corporation you can't stand and/or hate. Personally, I honestly can't imagine the US without corporations or businesses; it'd be a different type of country without them. Corporations are problematic very often and have less support than we'd hope (a majority of the country, nearly 80%, is not confident in big business[304]), but even still, businesses are undeniably here to stay.

---

[303] Ellen Terrell. When a quote is not (exactly) a quote: The Business of America is Business Edition. Library of Congress (2019).

"Bitch! I'm that, I'm that, I'm that bi-bi-bitch
I don't ask for forgiveness or permission
If I want it I'mma fuckin' go get it
On the court all by myself no competition
Y'all be mad about me like I never listen
Uh, I'm the big boss; Uh, I be spillin' sauce
Uh, I've got no fear of fallin' off; Uh, y'all niggas too soft
I'm that bitch, I'm that bitch; I'm that, I'm that, I'm that
I'm that bitch, I'm that bitch; I'm that, I'm that, I'm that
I'm that bitch, I'm that bitch; I'm that, I'm that, I'm that
I'm that bitch, I'm that bitch; I'm that, I'm that, I'm that. Bitch"

"The 'Corporate' Problem"

---

[304] id.

INTRODUCTION: SO WHAT? I'M A CORPORATE & SOCIAL LAW STUDENT; GET OVER IT AND YOURSELF

ARGUMENTS WITH FRIENDS OVER "CORPORATIONS"

CORPORATIONS IN GENERAL

    GENERAL ARGUMENTS FOR CORPORATIONS

    GENERAL ARGUMENTS AGAINST CORPORATIONS

A "CONSERVATIVE SOCIALIST" IDEOLOGY

CONCLUSION: BUSINESS IS THE HEARTBEAT OF AMERICA, JUST TO BE HONEST, BUT...

Fast, I'm coming in fast (uh-huh); First place, you coming in last (that's right)

I'm hitting that, hitting that gas; I'm hitting that, hitting that ass (my body)

I'm coming in fast (uh-huh); First place, you coming in last

I'm hitting that, hitting that gas; I'm hitting that, hitting that

Locomotion; We causing a commotion

I put it in, I put it in, I put it in motion; I put it in, I put it in, I put it in motion

Locomotion; We causing a commotion

Iciest bitch in the whole damn land; I hit the road in an all-white Lam'

I keep a fresh set up on my hands; You don't like me, but you on my 'Gram

How you look, how you look, how you sound, ho?; I'm a boss, I'm a brat, hard to handle

I'm a real life mood, a real life muse; Got some pretty-ass toes in my sandals

I can't help, I was born like this; Ain't my fault that you want my drip

Little bitter bitch could have been my friend; Now you gotta listen while I pop my shit"

-- Saweetie

INTRODUCTION: SO WHAT? I'M A CORPORATE & SOCIAL LAW STUDENT; GET OVER IT AND YOURSELF

Most people, when I tell them (which is rare) that I study corporate law in addition to socially driven law, they are often a) put off, b) wondering why I study corporations, and c) decently snarky about their disdain for corporations. Corporations are a toss-up to me though, and I think many, many people have the same sentiment towards these entities. So, I take it with a grain of salt when people are, a) b) and c), and often will add that I need to learn the corporate world if I want to change it. But I don't think corporations are all bad. I think they are simply needing to be bettered but a superbly valuable asset to the culture of the states.

So, so what I'm a corporate law student. Get over it.

ARGUMENTS WITH FRIENDS OVER "CORPORATIONS"

I've had a few frustrating conversations with friends about corporations. I think so many people are anti-corporation, but they use all types of products and services from corporations. What an oxymoronic issue.

Yes, corporations can be evil, manipulative, poorly run, abusive, and all the like, but to totally ignore all the good things corporations do is somewhat ignorant. The products and services afforded to us by corporations are so intriguing, and I think many people miss the point that while corporations are often pieces of work, they also are (collectively) way important to the continued brilliance of people in this country and world. As Mike Moffatt for Thought Co. outlines:

> Large companies can supply goods and services to a greater number of people, and they frequently operate more efficiently than small ones. In addition, they often can sell their products at lower prices because of the large volume and small costs

per unit sold. They have an advantage in the marketplace because many consumers are attracted to well-known brand names, which they believe guarantee a certain level of quality.[305]

So, corporations really run the gambit of good and bad (just like us humans). One might want to think about the absolute powerhouse corporations are in order to break them down and see what the actual benefit of them is, or rather, critique them. My mentor mentioned that corporations came up with the COVID-19 vaccine, so they definitely do some type of good, at least some of the time.

CORPORATIONS IN GENERAL

Corporations are often bad and evil in many ways. Think about things like Amazon working their employees to death, Walmart not paying its workers a livable wage, the countless number of fast-food jobs that don't allow people to make enough to house and feed themselves[306], etc.[307] But companies also do a significant amount of good, which is hard to ignore. Amazon delivers much needed supplies to anyone in a matter of a few days (with a Prime subscription), Walmart allows people to shop for things at a massive discount, and we all love driving through fast-food

---

[305] Mike Moffatt. Corporations in the United States. Thought Co. (2020).
[306] Information from a general knowledge of companies with dangerous practices.
[307] There is also a plethora of articles that describe the evilness of corporations... Here are four of them:
https://www.tampabay.com/news/business/corporate/from-bad-to-baddest-the-ten-nastiest-corporations-of-the-moment/2295964/
https://www.cracked.com/pictofacts-2171-evil-things-huge-companies-have-done
https://slate.com/technology/2020/01/evil-list-tech-companies-dangerous-amazon-facebook-google-palantir.html
https://www.thetoptens.com/most-evil-companies/

places for our quick meals. There are certainly upsides and downsides to the nature of corporations.

As the Atlantic points out: "Large corporations are vilified in a way that obscures the innovation they spur and the steady jobs they produce."[308] The article continues on to point out many fascinating logical inferences about the way people feel about business (big and small) and the relative facts about corporations. One of the best points is that:

> In 2015, small enterprises were four times more likely to lay off their workers than large ones. Workers employed by large firms also earned more—on average, 54 percent more than workers at small companies. Companies with more than 500 employees offer 2.5 times more paid leave and insurance benefits and 3.9 times more in retirement benefits than workers at firms with fewer than 100 employees. Large firms are also more likely to be unionized, and they employ a greater share of women and minorities than small firms do, making Big Business an unlikely enemy of progressives.[309]

There are also, generally, good corporations out there. Hannah Durbin from the company *Classy* outlines nine in her article, and I touch on my favorite five[310]:

Google
Google, in many opinions does well because of its environmental awareness, treatment of employees, and general contribution to the world. The company has been working on its carbon footprint (aiming to be carbon-free by 2030) and upping the awareness of other companies as it relates to their environmental impact. Finally, "[from] employee gift matching, to paid time off for volunteering,

---

[308] Atkinson & Lind. Is Big Business Really that Bad? The Atlantic (2018).
[309] id.
[310] Hannah Durbin. 9 Socially Conscious Companies to Model This Year. Classy (2021).

Google inspects nearly every part of their business with a social impact lens."[311]

Ben & Jerry's
As Durbin outlines:

> Ice cream tastes just a little sweeter when you know the makers work to promote safe, socially responsible ingredients and business practices. Since the 1980s, Ben & Jerry's has supported a number of important causes, many of which are directly tied to the business of making ice cream.[312]

Ben & Jerry's has fought against growth hormones used in cows, worked to encourage employees and others to better their communities, given social justice program grants, and fought against racism. "Ben & Jerry's impact is then further amplified by the Fairtrade social premium, an additional amount of money paid on top of the fair price that farmers receive."[313]

LEGO

LEGO is another company that is, at least, aiming toward some type of social awareness. Durbin details this saying:

> The LEGO Group is one of the most notable examples of how social responsibility can be an incredible asset to a well-known brand... In September of 2020, the LEGO Group announced that they were set to invest $400 million over the next three years to support their social responsibility and sustainability efforts... by the end of 2025, they are

---
[311] id.
[312] id.
[313] id.

going to start by phasing out single use plastic bags and installing additional solar panels on all factories... By 2022, the LEGO Group is also aiming to reach eight million children around the world annually with learning through play. In collaboration with the LEGO Foundation, UNICEF, Save the Children, and local partners, the team is working to scale up programs that give children the opportunity to develop life-long skills.[314]

Warby Parker

Warby Parker is famous for their "We'll send you 5 pairs to pick from" business model. Though, their social justice model is another great thing about them, as they also provide glasses to those that are in need.[315] Durbin adds to this idea stating:

> Through their Buy-A-Pair, Give-A-Pair program, Warby Parker makes a monthly donation to their nonprofit partners, such as VisionSpring, to bring prescription eyewear to people in developing countries. The company has distributed more than eight million pairs of glasses since its start in 2010. As of April 1, 2020, a portion of purchases will additionally go toward personal protective equipment and preventative health supplies for healthcare workers and communities in need.[316]

Microsoft

Microsoft is yet another shining example of a company dedicated to doing good in the world. Durbin outlines this saying:

---

[314] id.
[315] id.
[316] id.

> Microsoft changed the way the world works, studies, and plays with their computers and software. But their ambitions go far beyond the screen. The company... began its giving program in 1983 when the fledgling company raised $17,000 for charity. As their CSR web page explains, Microsoft's giving program has not only given time (employees in the U.S. volunteered more than 750,000 hours for nonprofits in 2020 alone), but also cash. In fiscal year 2020, the program raised over $221 million for nonprofits.

This list could have many more companies and many of them are indeed Top 9 or 10 material. Many companies do in fact do good for the world, though people certainly have a right to be skeptical.

Furthering the idea of corporate social responsibility, here is a link to the 2019 Aflac graphic (https://www.aflac.com/docs/about-aflac/csr-survey-assets/2019-aflac-csr-infographic-and-survey.pdf) that goes over many corporate social responsibility statistics and inferences that include:

- Purpose v. Profit
- Social/Business Impact
- Scrutiny & Forgiveness
- Generational Differences
- Expectations
- Bad Behavior
- Many Other Stats & Figures[317]

Businesses being "good" or "bad" is a tough debate. Though, given the research, perhaps corporations are not the worst thing in the world (though they could be bettered of course).

---

[317] Aflac. 2019 Corporate Social Responsibility Report. Aflac (2019)

GENERAL ARGUMENTS FOR CORPORATIONS

"Advantages of a corporation include personal liability protection, business security and continuity, and easier access to capital."[318]

Other advantages include:

Competition: Businesses spur competition in the world and keep the world "a turnin.'" The American Dream is built on the ideas of manifest destiny and competition, and that's what businesses seem to do/provide. [319]

Global Stability: Put frankly: the world is better off as a whole with business deals spurring global conversations, innovations, and the like. Many companies are multinational and thus might have employees all over the world working toward a similar goal. This is, arguably, beneficial for the world.[320]

People-Backed Corporations: Behind the corporation and its ideals is almost always a person or group of people. Investors, directors, employees, and owners all benefit from, and are usually the backbone of the corporation.[321]

People are Protected: The limited liability of corporations makes it the company's problem, usually, rather than the direct employees or other members of the corporation. This is highly

---

[318] Skye Schooley. Pros and Cons of Forming a Corporation. Business News Daily (2020).
[319] Up Counsel. Corporate Personhood. Up Counsel (2021).
[320] id.
[321] id.

important for the sake of people being able to guide the business in a safe and sustainable manner.[322]

Inclusion in Society: People working for companies allows them to work, live, and thrive in terms of being in the world. Yes, there are lots of problems with this argument, but corporations clearly employ a ton of people worldwide and oftentimes enable them to live a better life than without a job.[323]

To add, *The Economist* writer K.N.C. gives these powerful things that would not exist without corporations:

Without business we would not have:

* Ships, trains, and cars

* Electricity, lighting, and heating equipment

* Most of our food supply

* Most of our lifesaving pharmaceuticals

* Clothes for our children

* Our telephones and smartphones

* The books we love to read

* The ability to access, more or less immediately, so much of the world's online information

And let's not forget your paycheck. "Meeting payroll," to invoke a now old-fashioned phrase, is nothing less than a heroic act.[324]

So, again, there are benefits to corporations.

---

[322] id.
[323] id.
[324] K.N.C. Why we should embrace big business. The Economist (2019).

GENERAL ARGUMENTS AGAINST CORPORATIONS

"Disadvantages of a corporation include it being time-consuming and subject to double taxation, as well as having rigid formalities and protocols to follow." (Business News Daily).

Other disadvantages include:

Businesses Being "Real": The weird conundrum that businesses are people, just not "natural" people is a distinction that is strange to many. The idea that a business is its own distinct person could easily be construed as disrespectful to actual people and in its most basic form: a lie for the sake of business.[325]

Lack of Morality: The lack of morality of corporations is often atrocious. This must be bettered in America in so many ways (pay, environmental-impact, treatment of employees, mental health time off).[326] My mentor sent me an article about a pregnant Amazon worker that lost her child duet to Amazon's condition. This is terrible, but often the typical nature of tough-to-work-for companies.[327]

Corporate Personhood is Silly in Many Ways: The analysis of this by Up Counsel is kind of funny but very true. They say:

> A big part of personhood is feelings. Businesses have no feelings because they are not people. A business can't live. It can't die. Businesses do not feel love, get

---

[325] Up Counsel. Corporate Personhood. Up Counsel (2021).
[326] id.

[327] Lauren Gurley. Amazon Denied a Worker Pregnancy Accommodations. Then She Miscarried. VICE (2021).

married, or have children. If a business is not alive, then it is not a person and does not deserve personhood.[328]

Businesses are Money-Driven: Businesses (save nonprofits and social entrepreneurships, etc.) usually have a main (but not only) goal of making money. Thus, most businesses are money-driven and money-first, which often creates a lot of problems, especially in terms of immorality.[329] Amazon is yet another good ("bad") example here.

Corruption of Big Business: Big business can yield a ton of corruption, unjust enrichment, abuse of power, and the like.[330] Also, money corrupts people, and corporations are a prime example of such.

Environmental Damage: Corporations are known to damage the environments they are in, that is no secret at all, and is the reason for the plethora of regulations in industries. *Future of Working* provides this analysis on how corporations can be especially damaging to developing countries:

> Most developing countries do not have the same level of regulation and oversight that the developed world maintains to protect the environment. When these firms decide to do business in the international market, they are subject to local laws – not the ones that govern their domestic headquarters – when working to obtain raw materials.[331]

Obviously, environmental damage is a factor here.

---

[328] id.
[329] id.
[330] Future of Working. <u>19 Advantages and Disadvantages of Multinational Corporations</u>. Future of Working (2021).
[331] id.

Overworked Employees: Many companies overwork their employees. Personally, I worked as a tutor for a company that wanted us working a minimum of 25 hours a week, which is a lot of students and a ton of unpaid prep time, while I was a full-time student. I tried and tried to communicate to them, but it was brutal because they kept adding and adding students to my already overworked load.

High Stress & Low-Paid Work Environments: Both high stress environments and low-pay are significant downsides to corporations, who often profits to the general wellbeing of their employees. Many, many companies fall under this reasoning flaw.

A "CONSERVATIVE SOCIALIST" IDEOLOGY

I believe in the institutions: law, education, business, culture, etc. I am skeptical of how things are often run, accomplished, dealt with, etc. oftentimes, which is why I study all these subjects to hopefully better them throughout the things I do in my life.

I also believe that the institutions are meant to serve the people. If an institution doesn't work for people or for the benefit of people, I'm pretty skeptical of it. Institutions are for the betterment of people in my mind.

I consider that to make me a conservative socialist, red and light blue. Say what you want about it, but I think I acknowledge both sides of all these arguments pretty damn well.

CONCLUSION: BUSINESS IS THE HEARTBEAT OF AMERICA, JUST TO BE HONEST, BUT...

Business is the heart of America and American capitalism. My mentor/professor included the President Calvin Coolidge quote which reads: "After all, the chief business of the American people is business. They are profoundly concerned with producing, buying, selling, investing and prospering in the world."[332] That's the analogy I love to think of: businesses here, there, and everywhere, that's the states I know. Small business, medium-size business, large corporations: all pumping much-needed blood to the people in this country. Nonprofits are also considered corporations, so, as my mentor mentioned to me, there is likely a company that does something you absolutely love/support for every corporation you can't stand and/or hate. Personally, I honestly can't imagine the US without corporations or businesses; it'd be a different type of country without them. Corporations are problematic very often and have less support than we'd hope (a majority of the country, nearly 80%, is not confident in big business[333]), but even still, businesses are undeniably here to stay.

"Bitch! I'm that, I'm that, I'm that bi-bi-bitch

I don't ask for forgiveness or permission

If I want it I'mma fuckin' go get it

On the court all by myself no competition

---

[332] Ellen Terrell. When a quote is not (exactly) a quote: The Business of America is Business Edition. Library of Congress (2019).

[333] id.

Y'all be mad about me like I never listen
Uh, I'm the big boss; Uh, I be spillin' sauce
Uh, I've got no fear of fallin' off; Uh, y'all niggas too soft
I'm that bitch, I'm that bitch; I'm that, I'm that, I'm that
I'm that bitch, I'm that bitch; I'm that, I'm that, I'm that
I'm that bitch, I'm that bitch; I'm that, I'm that, I'm that
I'm that bitch, I'm that bitch; I'm that, I'm that, I'm that. Bitch"

The 'Bureaucracy' Problem

TABLE OF CONTENTS

INTRODUCTION: "AGENCIES v. ADMINISTRATION"

THE RUNNING OF A FIRM

THE RUNNING OF AGENCIES

BURDENS ADMINISTRATIONS BEAR

CONCLUSION: "THE IMPACT OF BUREACACIES AFFECTS ACTUAL PEOPLE"

"Yachty, I might stop rappin' for this one reason:

If the feds hear this shit I'm doin' 100 seasons"

-- Tee Grizzley

"Tryna smoke the pain away, they lock us up for smoking

Put 'em on probation, lock you up if you ain't perfect

Victims of the system like a rain drop in the ocean

They closin' all the schools and all the prisons gettin' open"

-- Meek Mill

INTRODUCTION: "AGENCIES v. ADMINISTRATION"

I wanted to be a Social/Political and Corporate/Administrative focused MLS, and I sure was. Though, it is important to note that administrative law includes both administrative agencies and their going but also legal administration (the administration that runs firms). So: I studied both and they were both key in terms of my "generalist" style of study.

THE RUNNING OF A FIRM

Running a law firm is complex; legal professionals working in legal administration indeed have a difficult job/duty.

Legal administrators facilitate all of the following:

- Starting & Running Firms
- Getting & Retaining Clients
- Setting Fees
- Managing the Office & Employees
- Ethics & Professional Responsibility
- Resources & Advice
- Quality of Life for All Involved[334]

Again, this is tough work.

THE RUNNING OF AGENCIES

Agencies are a function of the government. They are, in effect, an arm or sect of the 3 branches of government (executive, judicial, legislative), and have elements or calls from each branch.

Agencies namely are concerned with

- Delegated Authority
- Political Controls
- Judicial Review
- Acquiring & Disclosing Public Info
- Administrative Process
- Due Process of Public, etc.
- Adjudication & Rulemaking
- Orders & Regulations[335]

---

[334] Jay Foonberg. How to Start & Build A Law Practice. 5 ABA (2004).
[335] Levin & Lubbins. Administrative Law in a Nutshell. 6 West Publishing (2017).

Complex stuff.

Agencies hold an emphasis on their procedures and actions affecting the public. Often, the administrative agencies emphasize case method as well. These agencies regulate industries, issue rules and order, are court-backed, and again, are a sect of the government branches. They are delegated powers by the branches and hold legislative and adjudicative power, mostly to protect the public and make rules for industries.[336]

Due process, rulemaking, and judicial review are thus key in understanding agencies.[337]

Public information and the acquisition/disclosing of such are also key.[338]

BURDENS ADMINISTRATIONS BEAR

Administrative agencies and legal administrations have plenty of burdens. The burdens for legal administrators are listed in the 2nd section of this work (The Running of a Firm) and here are some of the burdens administrative agencies face:

- Political Access
- Race Relations
- Diversity, Equity & Inclusion
- Abortion Restrictions
- Affordable Medical Care
- Medicare & Medicaid
- SNAP & EBT
- Social Security
- Business Regulation & Upkeep

---

[336] William Funk. Administrative Law. 3 Wolters Kluwer (2009).

[337] id.

[338] Id.

- Banking & Securities
- Safety & Community Outreach
- Pandemics & Outbreaks[339]

So, yeah, administrative agencies, like legal administrators, deal with a ton.

CONCLUSION: "THE IMPACT OF BUREACACIES AFFECTS ACTUAL PEOPLE"

Bureaucracies, especially governmental ones, affect a multitude of people in a variety of ways. I don't quite think that government agencies are doing enough to solve America's core problems, though I know the work is complex. For me, I think of COVID times and going through the SSI system as a disabled person and I think: "geez the government does a lot, but also could and should be doing a lot more, especially for marginalized folx."

So, I'll leave you with that idea.

"They say, "Time is money", but money can't make no time (make no time)
Sometimes it's sunny, but sometimes it don't shine (no, it don't shine)
And life is a bitch, but sometimes it's alright (ooh, it's alright)
So I'ma let go of things I can't control"

-- Justin Bieber

---

[339] Herd & Moynihan. Administrative Burden. Russell Sage Foundation (2018).

"You're the reason there's no whiskey
Anywhere inside this house
You're the reason all my friends know I don't go downtown
You're the reason I hate champagne
Never used to turn it down
You're the only thing I want when one drop hits my mouth
Baby, you're the reason
I quit drinking"

-- Kelsea Ballerini

"The 'Contractual Obligations' Problem"

INTRODUCTION: "I DONE SEEN A LOT OF MOVIES 'BOUT ARTISTS BEING ABUSED BY THE INDUSTRY"

THE PROBLEM WITH UNFAIR CONTRACTS

THE THINGS "TO BE CARRIED ON" WITH CONTRACTUAL OBLIGATIONS

CONCLUSION: "I REFUSE TO BE USED AND ABUSED, ESPECIALLY BY A CONTRACT"

"Yeah, riding with my billionaire homie, I got the Glock up on me; He always asking me why I got it? Been tryna hide it from him

He tell me, "Why don't you get some security? You got a lot of money"; But I can't get this shit out my heart that took my father from me

Shit, do you know the feeling of success?; When you young and you black but you stressed and you blessed

And you gotta wake up every single morning, do your best; And when you get your cake up niggas gon' try you on the 'net

I had to switch way up 'cause I can't die by my respect; I got kids I gotta feed, I got a momma that can't grieve

When it was slow and niggas left, I made my mind up, I can't leave;
Plus homie doing life, shit, I got guys that got free

Juveniles don't get no life at 17, he was 18; They gave him life so we gotta pray and believe

And try to squeeze on every resource that we know that he need; We must achieve; And once we see him we gon' go and succeed; The heart of Creed, I'm from Philly, nigga

From the balcony I see the fountain blue; Over the bridge is muddy waters, 'til your dreams come true

But I can have it all, I can have it (I can have it); I can have it all, I can have it (I can have it)

From the balcony I see the fountain blue; Over the bridge is muddy waters, 'til your dreams come true; But I can have it all, I can have it (I can have it); I can have it all, I can have it"

-- DJ Khaled, Meek Mill, & H.E.R.

INTRODUCTION: "I DONE SEEN A LOT OF MOVIES 'BOUT ARTISTS BEING ABUSED BY THE INDUSTRY"

So…. I've seen or heard of so many movies/documentaries/stories about artists (TLC, Motown Records, Tina Turner, Britney Spears, etc.) where the artists were exploited by unfair contracts or people. It's crazy.

You always hear about those crazy 360 music deals where artists have to pay all their own costs with their sales, which ends up being crazy rough for them.

If you don't believe me: I've referenced in the footnotes two articles that talk about artists being exploited by contracts.[340][341]

The point of this is: contracts very much do have the power to fuck people over.

This paper discusses issues with contracts and specifically unfair contracts.

THE PROBLEM WITH UNFAIR CONTRACTS

The problem with unfair contracts is that they are unfair but often can be enforced.

One great example of this is corporate arbitration. Many, many companies and the like will have you sign a contract (i.e., terms and conditions) that make you give up your right to sue them in an actual court over the product they are offering you, and rather, if you have a legal issue, you will be bound to taking it up with an arbitration court of their choosing (i.e., home cookin'). Good luck suing them in that court, by signing the agreement they offer you (which, in most all cases, is necessary to use their product or service) you have basically agreed to not sue them or basically settle for little to nothing if you actually do have a real and valid issue. [342] You could not use their service, but

---

[340] Debra Kelly. <u>INSANE TIMES MUSIC ARTISTS WERE SCREWED OVER BY THEIR RECORDING COMPANIES.</u> Grunge (2020).

[341] Eden Gordon. <u>Before Taylor Swift: 6 Artists Who Were Screwed Over by Their Labels.</u> Pop Dust (2019).

[342] My professor for this research asked if I had any statistics about corporations v. laypeople, and I don't. But what I do have is the background of being the son of a corporate lawyer, and I once read an article in the LA

who isn't using a variety of platforms/services these days? This is an unfair but very much enforced practice in the corporate world.[343]

Wild right?

THE THINGS TO BE CARRIED ON" WITH CONTRACTUAL OBLIGATIONS

Another extreme example of contracts is the "shit to be carried on" with contractual obligations. Think of your job or a terrible job you had. In order to not get fired and make the money for being there: there were plenty of contractual obligations you have to carry on (listen to your boss, do your job, treat the customers well, etc.). That's a whole lot for anyone, save those accustomed to taking orders, so think of contractual obligations as the worst things about your job and the fact that you have to do them or else you won't make dat money.[344] A great example of this is working in the retail/customer service industry. Often, people can be disrespectful, loud, inappropriate, and all the like; yet, because the retail/customer service worker is "working", they have to act cool, calm, collected, and disrespected. How relatable is that struggle these days with Karens running wild all over the country. The remedies for this could be vast (barring the "Karen from the store," disaster-type pay, mental health time off, etc.).

Times about Disney using its "Sith/Stormtroopers" army to bully their way into all that they have now. So... ya know, I've definitely seen some corporate domination in my time.
[343] Steph. 10 Funny Terms and Conditions That'll Teach You A Lesson. Chango (2021).

[344] Information from experiences in the working world.

233

The systems we have are so intriguing due to their seemingly, intensely strange conundrums.

CONCLUSION: "I REFUSE TO BE USED AND ABUSED, ESPECIALLY BY A CONTRACT"

Being sued for breach is nowhere near as bad as being used and abused by a contract. Here's what Legal Match says about abusive contracts:

> A contract can be unconscionable if it involves duress, undue influence, or unequal bargaining power. Most abusive contracts are unconscionable because of unequal bargaining power- one party took advantage of the other party's lack of knowledge, experience, or resources.
>
> In some cases, an abusive contract may also be voided because the subject matter of the contract is illegal: Illegal contracts usually involve activities that are prohibited under state or federal laws, for example: gambling, employing a minor, or agreeing to enforce discriminatory employment policies/practices.[345]

So yeah, I'm definitely not going to be controlled by an abusive contract even if I signed it: point blank. My mentor said this about this paper's directions:

> So, contracts that compel you to do a crime are invalid. Maybe this should be extended to contracts that require being subject to abuse? Or instead of waiting to be sued and then countersuing, maybe a declaratory review of a contract prior to breaching it to determine if you can get it changed or cancelled?

This could certainly be an option. The definition of "unconscionable" in terms of contracts could easily play into this defense of a breach-activity. Very keen and very true.

Countersuing for being required to do bullshit activities (i.e., things that involve harassment, exploitation, lewdness, etc.) is also, often, an option.

---

[345] Legal Match Staff. Abusive Contracts. Legal Match (2021).

I'm not gonna be bound by a ridiculous contract, even if I signed it. You might feel the same.

_____
_____

"And he a rap nigga, say he independent, But I got 'em in a 360"

-- City Girls

"The 'Law Firm' Problem"

TABLE OF CONTENTS

INTRODUCTION: THIS PAPER IS ABOUT SMALLER LAW FIRMS

LAWYERS NEED TO PAY BACK STUDENT LOANS

THE COSTS OF A RUNNING A FIRM ARE NOT CHEAP

THE MANY LACKINGS

    RESOURCES

DOUBLE-CHECKING/CONFIRMING INFORMATION

PEOPLE

DELEGATION ABILITIES

EXPERTISE

LOCATION

OFFICE FURNISHINGS

CAPITAL

PRIVATE INVESTIGATORS

ETC., ETC., ETC.

LAWYERS CAN CHARGE A PREMIUM FOR THEIR EXPERTISE

CONCLUSION: "LAWYERS GOTTA MAKE IT TOO, I GUESS"

"Ballin' is a drug,

That I don't mind abusin'"

-- Chalie Boy

INTRODUCTION: "THIS PAPER IS ABOUT SMALLER LAW FIRMS"

This paper refers to the practice of smaller firms (1-30 people or so). There are other papers about large law firms in this thesis, though this paper is about the troubles of funding a small law firm and the subsequent large fees that lawyers charge. This paper basically explains why hiring a lawyer from a small law firm is still expensive due to the myriad costs it takes to run a firm.[346]

LAWYERS NEED TO PAY BACK STUDENT LOANS

The first reason why lawyers charge a lot is because most have student loans to repay. On average, 3 years in law school costs future lawyers something around 100k – 200k, and "even for the least expensive option, in-state public school, the cost over three years is $84,792".[347]

This is a high cost to pay, so lawyers have to work for a high price because of the debt from law school.

THE COSTS OF A RUNNING A FIRM ARE NOT CHEAP

---

[346] All information in this paper comes from 3 sources: 1) Jay Foonberg's How to Start and Build a Law Practice, 2) My "Law as a Business" law course at DU Sturm and 3) my dad's brief insights about costs firms incur.
[347] College Ave Student Loans. How Much Does Law School Cost? Average Law Degree Tuition & Costs. College Ave Student Loans (2020).

Additionally, small law firms have a lot of costs. The next sections detail the lackings or havings of firms and why that results in high legal costs.

THE MANY LACKINGS

Lackings or havings can be make or break for any small firm, and the next sections detail why: there are tons of costs for a small firm.

RESOURCES

Resources of all kinds could be short (monetary, investigatory, time, womanpower, etc.). This is an important start.

DOUBLE-CHECKING/CONFIRMING INFORMATION

Having law books or WestLaw subscriptions and the womanpower to locate and confirm information can be tough and timely (meaning more money charged in hours).

PEOPLE

Small firms don't have a ton of people, so cases/expertise/training must be diverse, but probably won't be as "expert" in many things, save if the small firm has a specific focus.

DELEGATION ABILITIES

With few people, delegation is tough, which means a higher cost for the time of the lawyer handling a case.

EXPERTISE

Again, expertise can be tough if the small firm isn't specialized, and even still there are less people around to learn from, seemingly less professional development (as opposed to corporate lawyers at big firms), and the like.

LOCATION

Location is a big cost (often a big initial barrier), and keeping it cooled/heated/with coffee/etc. is expensive and results in higher costs for law services.

OFFICE FURNISHINGS

Furnishing the office is another big start-up cost.

CAPITAL

Keeping capital for all sorts of things (entertaining clients, travel, hiring investigators, paying salaries, etc.) is uber-important and is a resultant cost on the consumer.

PRIVATE INVESTIGATORS

Investigators who confirm and detail information are not cheap either, but certainly a necessary cost of practicing law.

ETC., ETC., ETC.

Other costs could be numerous too; this is by no means an exhausted list.[348]

LAWYERS CAN CHARGE A PREMIUM FOR THEIR EXPERTISE

Finally, and arguably most importantly, lawyers have a specialized and lucrative set of skills that allow them to charge a premium for their service, especially considering lawyers hold a monopoly on the practice of law. All this adds up to one hell of a legal bill for clients.

CONCLUSION: "LAWYERS GOTTA MAKE IT TOO, I GUESS"

I guess lawyers gotta make it too though... And I guess we're all in this American Rat Race to avoid poverty and other aspects of not making enough money. Sad, but true.

_____
_____

"Pride is the devil

---

[348] All information in these sections from the aforementioned 3 main sources.

Think it's got a hold on me,

Pride is the devil

It left so many RIP's...

Slowly realizin' what the root of all my problems be,

Got me feelin' different when somebody say they proud of me"

-- J. Cole

"The 'Big Law Firm' Problem"

TABLE OF CONTENTS

INTRODUCTION: "THE GENERAL LANDSCAPE OF 'LAW' & 'LAWYERS' AND THE PROBLEM OF BIG LAW"

A TURN TOWARD BIG LAW

    THE PROBLEM OF LARGE LAW FIRM COMPETITION TOURNEYS

    THE ISSUE OF DIVERSITY ETHICS FOR LARGE FIRMS

    THE ISSUE OF NEW-AGE TOURNEYS NOT WORKING FOR QUEER & DISABLED LAW PROFESSIONALS SPECIFICALLY

WHY THAT IS A DEEPER ISSUE FOR CULTURE

CONCLUSION: "A REMINDER OF WHY LAW IS THE LEAST DIVERSE FIELD IN THE U.S."

"Blood sweat tears; Ace Hood (I do it)

Uh! Another day, another dollar; Every twenty four I'm thinking money in the power
Bills due, money runnin' low; Plus my cousin lost her mind and had an overdose
Way too many problems got me stressed out; What you do when you've got seven days to move out
Go 'n' get it, go 'n' get it, go 'n' get it; I'm out here chasin' cream
Go 'n' get it, go 'n' get it, go 'n' get it; Need it by any means"

-- Ace Hood

INTRODUCTION: "THE GENERAL LANDSCAPE OF LAW & "LAWYERS AND THE PROBLEM OF BIG LAW""

The general landscape of lawyers is non-diverse.

In the 2019 NALP Report on Diversity in US Law Firms (all law firms, not just large): people of color accounted for around a quarter of attorneys, 45% of lawyers were women (about 15% of lawyers were WOC), about 5% of lawyers were black and the same for LatinX lawyers, 10% of partners were of color (around 4% of equity partners), women were 1/4th of partners (though only about 12% of equity partners), 3% of lawyers were queer (2% of partners), there was a "scarce" amount of disabled lawyers (all counts less than 2%)[349]. Truly depressing numbers in many senses. You would hope for the percentage of lawyers in various categories would represent

---

[349] NALP. 2019 NALP Report. National Association for Law Placement (2020).

their general populations in America (queer at 10% not 3%, women at 50% at all levels, etc.).

In a 2020 report, the ABA stated that:

> Lawyers who either identify as having disabilities or who identify as LGBTQ+ report experiencing both subtle and overt forms of discrimination at their workplaces, with common reports of subtle but unintentional biases, according to a first-of-its-kind national study released July 14 by the American Bar Association, in collaboration with the Burton Blatt Institute at Syracuse University.[350]

Some key findings from the study were:

> **Prevalence of subtle biases.** Almost 4 of 10 (38.5%, 1,076) of all responses reported perceptions or experiences of subtle but unintentional biases. More than 1 in 5 respondents (21.7%, 607) noted the experience of subtle and intentional biases.
>
> **Prevalence of mental health conditions.** One-quarter (25.0%, 830) of respondents reported a health impairment, condition or disability. Of the 1,374 total responses, almost one-third (30.8%) reported a mental condition, which could include depression, anxiety and cognitive conditions such as attention deficit hyperactivity disorder (ADHD), autism and traumatic brain injury.
>
> **Variations in bias and intersectional identities.** Approximately 16.6% of the lawyers responding identified as lesbian, gay or bisexual, and 0.4% identified their sexual orientation as open. Of 67 lawyers who were women and identified as LGB with a health condition, slightly more than half (52.2%, 35) reported they had experienced discrimination in their workplaces. Lawyers with a health condition or impairment and who identify as a person with a disability reported experiencing more overt forms of discrimination, such as bullying and harassment, as compared to people who do not have such conditions. Attitudinal biases and structural barriers may be even more challenging for those with multiple identities that intersect.

---

[350] ABA. ABA study: Disabled, LGBTQ+ lawyers face discrimination. ABA (2020).

Bias mitigation strategies. When asked to report strategies that were especially effective in lessening either overt or subtle forms of bias or discrimination in their workplaces, fewer than half (46%) reported finding effective strategies. Mentoring within (20.5%, 1,490) and outside (18.4%, 1,335) their organizations was reported as an effective mitigation strategy.

Requests for workplace accommodation. More than one-quarter of all respondents (28.4%, 807) reported requesting a workplace accommodation from their organization. Of the 730 respondents who reported a health condition, impairment or disability, fewer than half (42.9%, 313) had requested an accommodation.[351]

Timothy Clary had (pre)echoed these in 2019 for Bloomberg Law, stating that queer people still faced barriers that included:

- Low numbers in firms
- Being "out" dynamics
- Homophobia/Transphobia
- Trans struggles
- Non-welcoming cultures/policies/etc.
- Poor treatment or treatment as different rather than equal

The question of whether large firms or small firms are better (in terms of treatment) for queer people, though, seems to be a debate of numbers (and isolation) or culture (good and bad). Perhaps small firms provide worse cultures for queer people with the likeliness for singling out and personal business to be a factor, though small cultures could be much more queer-inclined than a numbers-jumble big firm. This is certainly a debate in the field.

Though, going with this: big law firms can often be hyperbolized versions of these numbers (shockingly sad as

---

[351] id.

that seems). Experiences (and oftentimes numbers too) tell this story (and the reasons why it happens) well.

Stephanie Russell for Bloomberg Law reminds us to remember that real changes are really only as recent as 2010 or 2015 (Obama era, marriage rights, workplace rights, trans progress, bisexuality/pansexual/asexual/nonbinary/etc. awareness) She eloquently states:

> Transgender and nonbinary attorneys in the legal industry face especially high risk of experiencing bias at work and fear that coming out could damage their careers. And LGBTQ attorneys of color say they experience additional marginalization and discrimination at work because of their race.[352]

She also reminds us that coming out in a law firm is still a major issue. She enlists stats to show how tough it is to be the "queer one" at work (because there won't be many given the numbers):

> Only 1% of U.S. lawyers identified as LGBT in 2004. Fifteen years later, that number tripled, according to the National Association of Law Placement. And among the newest generation in Big Law, the numbers are higher. In NALP's 2019 survey of U.S. law firms, only 2% of partners identified as LGBT, whereas 4% of associates and nearly 7% of summer associates did.[353]

She continues with a series of interviews that show there are still a lot of barriers for queer people (notably trans people and LGBTQ+ folks of color) in big law:

> Many Big Law firms now tout their inclusiveness through creating affinity groups, filing amicus briefs in favor of gay

---

[352] Stephanie Russell-Kraft. It's Gotten Better to Be LGBTQ in Big Law, but Struggles Remain. Bloomberg Law (2020).

[353] id.

rights causes, and holding annual Pride celebrations. But extra hurdles still remain in the workplace for some LGBTQ lawyers.

"Big Law is much more inclusive than probably most other industries for gays and lesbians, but I think that for our transgender and nonbinary communities, there are still a lot of barriers." said Cannon. "In some ways we as a society are just starting to educate ourselves on the other groups within the LGBTQ community."

Claire Bow, former executive director of the Texas State Office of Risk Management, began practicing law in 1983 but did not feel comfortable coming out as transgender until shortly before her retirement in 2014. "I just never saw a pathway for me to be out," said Bow. "I never felt safe enough that I could have come out in any of those workplaces."

Now a transgender rights activist, she said she knows others who have decided they don't want to come out or don't feel safe doing so.

Detailed statistics regarding transgender lawyers are scarce. In 2018, NALP reported 35 transgender graduates at 28 law schools. According to the organization, those graduates were twice as likely to work in public service, which includes jobs in government, public interest, and judicial clerkships, than in firms.

Kristen Prata Browde, co-chair of National Trans Bar Association and president of the LGBT Bar Association of Greater New York, said most of the other trans attorneys she knows work in advocacy or public service law. Browde said she knows of only two trans lawyers in Big Law above the associate level.

Part of the challenge, according to Browde, is that coming out as transgender can be a highly visible act, particularly for a mid-career attorney. "Somebody who says, I'm gay or I'm lesbian, if they choose to say it, they're going to look the same and nobody outside their immediate circle is going to have any idea," she said. "If you come out as trans, you oftentimes will look different from the day you walked in the door."

Lawyers of color who are also LGBTQ said they faced additional challenges and biases.

"Some of the most outspoken people and the most visible people [in the legal LGBTQ community] tend to be the White guys, and I don't necessarily find that there's a lot of empathy for the Black experience or being a person of color and being gay," said Bobbie Wilson, a litigation partner at Perkins Coie.

In 2019, only about 9.5% of U.S. law firm partners and 17% of all attorneys were people of color, according to NALP. Only about 2% of partners and less than 5% of associates were Black.

"You walk in the room and no one makes negative assumptions when you're the White guy in the suit," Wilson said. "But I walk into depositions sometimes and people think I'm the court reporter, sometimes the defendant."

Wilson said racism has been a much bigger problem for her in the law than homophobia. "It's almost as if they can't see past the brown to learn about the gay," she said.[354]

---

[354] id.

Russell communicates that her interviews of LGBTQ lawyers show "the legal industry still has progress to make, but many were encouraged by the newest generation of lawyers entering the profession."

Being authentically queer in big law is "more comfortable," though generational divides, a lack of support (especially from fellow queer folk), inclusivity with terms/pronouns/open-mindedness/etc., a needing to temper assumptions/stereotypes/generalizations, a needing to challenge uncomfortability/homophobia/transphobia/etc., a needing to engage in queer theory and dialogue in general, and not expecting queer folx and folx of color to "do a lot of the heavy lifting" are still major deficits faced for the queer community.[355]

One participant even said lessons in queerness and the like should be billable hours ▢.

Takeia Johnson outlines the difficulties that LGBTQ+ attorneys of color face. She says they face unique issues that include:
- Stigmatized identities
- Lack of materials/study on them
- The need for more work to be done for the communities
- Others understanding the issues first
- Essentialism (Minority or queer not both)
- Monolithic ideologies (LGBTQ+ people of color have the same experience)
- Coming out and being out
- Intersectionality issues[356]

---

[355] id.
[356] Takiea Johnson. LGBT Attorneys of Color in the Legal Profession: A Discourse on Inclusion. Federal Lawyer (2017).

She concludes with these four rationales (from the American Bar Association's Presidential Diversity Initiative) for more diverse legal profession spaces:

> **The Democracy Rationale:** Lawyers and judges have a unique responsibility for sustaining a political system with broad participation by all its citizens. A diverse bar and bench create greater trust in the mechanisms of government and the rule of law. Without a diverse bench and bar, the rule of law is weakened as the people see and come to distrust their exclusion from the mechanisms of justice.
>
> **The Business Rationale:** Business entities are rapidly responding to the needs of global customers, suppliers, and competitors by creating workforces from many different backgrounds, perspectives, skill sets, and tastes. Ever more frequently, clients expect and sometimes demand lawyers who are culturally and linguistically proficient. A diverse workforce within legal and judicial offices exhibits different perspectives, life experiences, linguistic and cultural skills, and knowledge about international markets, legal regimes, different geographies, and current events.
>
> **The Leadership Rationale:** Individuals with law degrees often possess the communication and interpersonal skills and the social networks to rise into civic leadership positions, both in and out of politics. Justice Sandra Day O'Connor recognized this when she noted in Grutter v. Bollinger27 that law schools serve as the training ground for such leadership and therefore access to the profession must be broadly inclusive.

The Demographic Rationale: Our country is becoming diverse along many dimensions, and we expect that the profile of LGBT lawyers and lawyers with disabilities will increase more rapidly. With respect to the nation's racial/ethnic populations, the Census Bureau projects that by 2042 the United States will be a "majority minority" country.[357]

I think that pointing toward these major diversity issues and really nailing down the sometimes-disastrous nature of these "large law firm" organizations, especially for "marginalized" LGBT+, in a variety of facets, is important for the study of fields in general (as it represents a top spectrum of "work" in the states, and thus, I, and perhaps many others, would hope for diversity in its ranks). This paper is also consistent with the larger work of my thesis about marginalization as related to legal issues/problems.

Law practice is again, non-diverse and law study looks only slightly better (with seemingly better numbers and environments on campuses rather than in a more high-stakes legal work environment) but brush that off as a cherry on top of a sundae with expired (like very expired) ice cream. It's painful to eat, to watch people eat, it stinks, and it's terrible.

Let's use that cherry and get new ice cream.

The ice cream of diversity and inclusion among lawyers. Ethnically, sexually, LGBT+ status, disability status, gender, class, and all the like.

---

[357] id.

Isn't that what law truly needs at this point in our 45-white, 1-black, 0-other-minority, 0-women Presidents history? Or our history of oppressing black, brown, poor people, women and others?

We can't ask for the simple change that, hey the little guy might actually have a chance** of being represented by someone that looks like him?

Is that too much to ask the all-mighty legal system?

I'm just saying....

It's a thought...

A TURN TOWARD BIG LAW

Turning to big law though, I'll start with being a corporate law-student (as corporations are big law's most prominent clients). "Big Law" is a hyper-competitive sect of law for lawyers going through law school, with separate academic tracks and separate job opportunities accordingly... I'd know I studied Corporate Law in my Master's (Social, of course, too though). Which, by the way... is a bit strange to tell people, as when you mention that you want to or in fact do study corporate law, may law students (public law, employment law, family law type) and people in general will scoff at you.

Also, your classes later on in your program (or throughout as an MLS student) are likely going to be significantly different than the types aforementioned, as will be career options, salary pay after grad school, work environment, competitiveness, etc. So... you're kind of sectioned off into corporate law, which is kind of wild.

And people know corporate lawyers make bank but work crazy hours and "sell their soul to the corporation";

it's all just kinda known in law school and even outside of it.... something to think about here in terms of big law.

The only thing that saved me from being a corporate "dick" is the fact that I'm half social half corporate in terms of distinction in the law school and plus I don't aim to be a corporate lawyer and I'm even offering criticisms such as this to go with it.

Basically: I'm different.

Big law is different too. And a different kind of "problem" in terms of the issues I am discussing in this legal thesis.

Big law firms engage in what Dianne Mallig and Dave Foster call "multidisciplinary practices," which enlist a plethora of lawyers, specializations, clienteles, even whole departments like accountants, MLS's, paralegals, and the like, that are robust and provide a ton of funds to the firm with the work provided. You can see how this gets massive: especially with tournaments for partner roles and partner roles themselves being highly competitive.[358]

Big law firms are also like big banks, which leads me to a resource that identifies a conversation about big banks and some questions about them. Those include:

- The issue of big corporations and big bans and the financial crisis of '08, '09
- The idea of "no more 'too-big-to-fail'" banks and corporations

---

[358] Dianne Molvig. Multidisciplinary Practices: Service Package of the Future. Wisconsin Lawyer (1999).
Dave Foster. Get Off My Turf! Attorneys Fight Accountants over whether to Allow Multidisciplinary Practice. Texas Tech Law Review (2000).

- The idea of being too big and powerful to actually help society, and whether or not at that point the organization should be broken up[359]

This should all be a bit scary/startling...

The third point in that list discusses whether or not these institutions can actually help society. This is, in part, discussed by giving back, which includes pro bono. According to Ellyn Josef, writing for the South Texas Law Review:

> There are many advantages for operating a pro bono program within a large law firm. However, with these advantages come some disadvantages. While these disadvantages are not significant enough to discourage large law firms from highlighting and building their pro bono programs, it is important to be aware of these issues when discussing pro bono programs in these large law firms.[360]

As she relates, large law firms have an ethical obligation to provide pro bono services, and can offer their lawyers (with it):

- Training and Professional Development
- Morale Boosters
- Client/Business Development
- Collaboration (with Law Schools, Businesses, etc.)
- Statements (such as Signature Projects)[361]

Though, as Malka Herman outlines:

> Law firms may promote pro bono because it allows lawyers to feel like they are doing good in the world. By creating a pro bono outlet, law firms can ensure that fewer attorneys leave

---

[359] Saltzman et. al. "A Spirited Conversation Assessing the Risks and Benefits of Big Firms". UNC School of Law (2012).
[360] Ellyn Josef. Is Bigger Better? South Texas Law Review (2010).
[361] id.

because they are tired of corporate work. The problem with compartmentalizing is that lawyers who engage in pro bono may not feel the need to think as critically about the ethics of their corporate practice as they might if they could not consider their pro bono work in the balance. This is not to say that every big law attorney practices law in a way that is morally problematic. Rather, engaging in a pro bono practice creates an opportunity for big law attorneys to avoid critically facing and owning their choices and any qualms that may arise in so doing.[362]

So, there are certainly a number of issues relating to the lawyers at large law firms, their treatment, their lifestyles, their being/decision-making, and all the like. Kaufman et. al. provide a segment on the problem of ethics for a corporate lawyer, which include the questions of:

- Best Interests (You or Corporation) Issues
- Coverups, Schemes, & Fraud Issues
- Partner/Higher-Ups Issues
- Complications & Competition Issues
- Duties to Client Issues[363]

Furthering that is an analysis of law firms in movies (in the early 2000's and on at least) and how they are depicted. This keen analysis states:

> Asimow [the author of the work] believes that the explanation for the rash of harshly negative big-firm movies lies both in the public's evident distaste for lawyers in general and law firms in particular and in the traditional anti-business theme in film narrative. He sketches the history of the big law firm and contends that the world of big firm law practice has swung sharply in the direction of a business model rather than the traditional professionalism model. Finally, Asimow contends that in several respects the depiction in contemporary films of

---

[362] Malka Herman. Creating a 'Great Pro Bono' Practice. California Law Review (2021).
[363] Kaufman et. al. Problems in Professional Responsibility for a Changing Profession. (Ch. 5 Pt. A). Carolina Academic Press (2017).

> large firm life and law practice is fundamentally on target. In particular, the treatment in the movies of lawyer life style, billing improprieties, and hardball litigation tactics appears to be essentially correct.[364]

This is a fascinating find in terms of public perception of law firms and lawyers in them even if dated a bit. Perhaps things have even hyperbolized since then.

Mental health in the field is certainly an issue too. Kent Halkett for the Tennessee Bar Journal describes this stating:

> Mental health issues challenge the legal profession's most valuable asset--the individual attorney...
>
> I have been a practicing attorney for nearly 40 years. I attempted suicide six years ago. Thankfully, I did not succeed.
>
> A recent survey asked thousands of practicing attorneys in the United States: "In your professional legal career, have you contemplated suicide?" Almost 17.9 percent of the respondents answered "Yes." It is hard to contemplate, much less completely "wrap your head around," that reality.
>
> A terrible secret is hiding in plain sight, but too often it is swept under the rug: lawyers, statistically, suffer from some form of mental illness at a rate much higher than society as a whole.
>
> That is a crisis.
>
> The law is an inherently stressful way to earn a living. The profession is now a business. Poor mental health is a medical condition. It is perpetuated in the law through a combination of shame, stress, status and stigma. Attorneys--who are excellent problem solvers by nature, education and training-- have not solved the mental health problem in their ranks. Why?
>
> The good news: attorneys with mental health challenges can thrive in the profession.

---

[364] Michael Asimow. Embodiment of Evil. SSRN (2001).

The legal profession needs to refocus its attention and resources on this crisis. Colleagues are suffering on a daily basis. The COVID-19 virus pandemic has disrupted the practice of law and increased stress levels. The time is now...

Numerous studies have been performed on the prevalence of alcohol, drugs and mental health problems among attorneys...

The ABA Study found that 19 percent of legal professionals in the United States reported symptoms of anxiety and 28 percent of practicing attorneys suffered from depression.7

The ALM Survey found that 64 percent of legal professionals feel anxiety, a huge increase from the results in the ABA Study just two years earlier. It found that 31 percent of attorneys feel depressed. In addition, generally, when asked, "Do you think the profession has had a negative effect on your mental health over time?--nearly three-quarters of the respondents in the ALM Survey (more than 74 percent) answered "Yes." Also, more than one out of six of the attorneys surveyed admitted to considering suicide.

Of course, and finally, there are issues of diversity in large law firms. Ronald Sangrund in "Can We Talk?" has a conversation with a number of law leaders in Colorado (where I wrote this thesis) about diversity, bias, and inclusiveness in the legal community in 2016. This was a big deal and was recent and is in a purple but often very liberal state. That means this is a nationwide issue that happens in "God's Country" and the "Devil's Country" alike.[365]

All that being said, I will attempt to explain the queer aspects of being a lawyer especially in terms as how it pertains to being in a large law firm setting.

Thus, this venture is an exploration of queer lawyers in terms of big law firms and perhaps generally (though, not quite the focus of this work, rather something

---

[365] Ronald Sangrund. Can We Talk? Colorado Lawyer (2016).

as a primer or introduction) in terms queer lawyers in the legal realm.

THE PROBLEM OF LARGE LAW FIRM COMPETITION TOURNEYS

In big law, there is a such thing as elastic tournaments, which are big law competitions for coveted partner positions. Galanter and Palay outline the fact that these tournaments started near the start of the 1900's and were "chaperones of enterprise" for corporations (their main and most profitable clients)[366]. They continue to outline the fact that the "modern firm" was heavily invested in "promotion to partner" tourneys in which inspired growth and restructuring of the firm with success. Firms would get better and better in their respective fields with the competitions giving way to massive amounts of growth[367].

Continuing this discussion of large firms, Henderson and Galanter, and Wilkins and Gulati suggested a new tournament in the late 1990's and early 2000's: the elastic tourney[368]. These tournaments at large firm largely resembled the prior tourneys, but with a few updates: 1) the Cravath systems of hiring the best students from the elite schools 2) the lessened ethics of law due to the competition, and 3) a hindrance for marginalized folks despite new system (CITE)

This new system allowed for more diverse routes than competitions for partner. Rather, firms turned toward

---

[366] Galanter & Palay. Why the Big Get Bigger. 76 VA. L Rev. 747 (1990).
[367] Id.
[368] Henderson & Galanter. "The Elastic Tournament". Indiana University (2008). Wilkins and Gulati. Reconceiving the Tournament of Lawyers.

more diversity with more paths for lawyers and law professionals to emerge and grow in the firm without the intense partner competition[369]. This updated tourney suggested a more cultural, less-economically-driven, and unfortunately less diverse (in people) system. Women, minorities, and young lawyers are having issues in this system despite its newer and perhaps better systems for firms[370]. This is saddening, and I look to explore, in this work, whether queer (and disabled) people face the same issues in these firms' elastic tournaments.

A recent article (from 2020) by John Morley expresses why large law firms collapse. They name a number of reasons: partner ownership, partners leaving, partner sensitivity to profits, personal liability, financial stress, human capital issues, the absence of hard assets, signaling [i.e., partners leaving, etc.], client loyalties, labor market, effect of size, and expansion[371]. Of this list, I would say that human capital issues, signaling, client loyalties, and the labor market could all be easily impacted by queer opposition or acceptance in the workplace, and thus, in this paper I will also discuss the treatment of queer people in large law firms and the effect of such.

OK. So, student perspective (a real non-lawyer confession especially considering I don't aspire to lawyer at this point in my life), this is wild! They compete and compete and compete; make partner and make huge decisions; still, compete, compete, and compete; many are weeded out along the way; the company grows dangerously; etc. etc. etc.

---

[369] Id.
[370] Id.
[371] John Morley. Why Large Law Firms Collapse. The Business Lawyer (2020).

Perhaps less with the new tourneys, but the system of associate-to-partner competition, this law firm system sounds like your law firm is on drugs, humbly. New high (partner), new high, new high (ALL WHILE CUTTING NON-WORTHY DRUGS), do the drugs to be as happy as the law firm can be (profits).

Your law firm, sir, much like your country[372], is on drugs.

I can't believe this isn't evaluated more bluntly than this, lawyers are smart enough to see this process going down, c'mon.

THE ISSUE OF DIVERSITY ETHICS FOR LARGE FIRMS

Bob Gordon's book review of *The Code of Capital* is a wonderful primer in Kristen Pistor's work that describes how lawyers are central to the system of capitalism as they code the assets of the world into capital for their clients.[373]

However, this review (and the book, which is detailed in my introductory paper on the "Theo-Foundations of Law" in this thesis) is great in explaining how lawyers "grease the wheels of capitalism" and ensure corporations "generations of wealth" by simply legal coding (the mixing of capital and law).[374] Truly deep stuff.

---

[372] REFERENCE TO DRUG WORK, "YOUR COUNTRY IS ON DRUGS"
[373] Bob Gordon. "Review of the Code of Capital". Jotwell (2020).

[374] id.

Anyhow, given those parameters: the ethics of large firms (who have major corporate clients) should be highly important to those firms. As William Wernz questions (and debates) out about the ethics of large firms:

- **"Is lawyering an unethical profession?"**
    - **Answering: What is an honorable profession?**
    - **Answering: Lawyers do have a moral code**
- "Is the 'typical' lawyer a liar?"
    - Answering: This is a lively debate (as ethics run heavy in law)
- "What are lawyer's sins?"
    - Answering: Mostly the ambiguity encouraging evil
- **"What are large law firms' sins?"**
    - **Answering; Mostly moral problems and issues (ethics are often lost in the shuffle it seems)**
    - **Answering: Furthering the "moneyed classes" and padded/excessive billing**
    - **Answering: Money making as potentially a dominant value in large firms**[375]

So, in terms of the bolded parts here: is lawyering unethical answered by "is anything ethical?" Ugh, c'mon Mr. Wernz that's terrible.

Also, large law firms' sins also look begrudgingly bad considering the scope of evil done and that could be done in the world. Also terrible. To add to this discussion,

---

[375] William Wernz. The Ethics of Large Firms. Georgetown Law Journal (2002).

there are, of course, "regulatory controls of law firms," which include:

- **REPUTATION (Personal [Attorneys] & Institutional [Firm at Large])**
- The Bar, Courts, & Judges
- Bureaucracy, Policies, & Routines
- Partner/Associate Dynamics
- Distinct Clienteles with Recurring & Novel Problems
- A Plethora of Attorney Options
- Specialization of Lawyers
- **SOLVING CONFLICTS & RISK MANAGEMENT**[376]

The first one and the last two are big here. The law is all about solving conflicts and risk management is key when handling corporate clients. Your reputation is built on these two major areas and is key in large law.

In the early 2000's David Wilkins wrote a paper discussing the "emerging role of ethics advisors, general counsel, and other compliance specialists (like today's DEI [Diversity, Equity, & Inclusion] officers and the like) at large law firms." This article described how:

> According to a recently-appointed general counsel, "A lot of law firms have a lot of problems they don't know about because there is no central repository for hearing them."10 From a regulatory standpoint, the emergence of in-house compliance specialists is a pivotal development. Research in other organizational contexts shows that such specialists tend to promote the development of compliance procedures within firms,11 and may play a leading role in defining industry standards for compliance.[377]

---

[376] Hazard & Schneyer. Regulatory Controls of Large Firms. Arizona Law Review (2002).
[377] David Wilkins. The Emerging Role of Ethics Advisors, General

This could be very important because pivotal players either in large firms (or schools, etc.) or contracted to be impactful in large firms could be highly influential in changing the climate for trans folks and queer folks of color. Especially considering that, that implementation of an officer, board, or other entities could be influential in hiring, promoting, and retaining quality queer legal talent, especially if there is a deficit to be made up for trans and queer folks of color.

Libby Adler brilliantly addresses the issue of the need for queer theory, discussion, and treatment to be diversified to all walks of queer life, not just gay men or gay marriage or homophobia. As Google Books describes of the book:

> Libby Adler offers a comprehensive critique of the mainstream LGBT legal agenda in the United States, showing how LGBT equal rights discourse drives legal advocates toward a narrow array of reform objectives that do little to help the lives of the most marginalized members of the LGBT community.[378]

The big issue here is "privileged problems" v. "actual problems" which perfectly describes LGBT+ treatment in big law (good for mainstream queer people but not marginalized queer folks). This is a tragic reality of big law.

The lack of diversity at big law firms is indeed a cultural problem, one that must be further looked into with things such as this work.

Counsel, and Other Compliance Specialists at Large Law Firms. Arizona Law Review (2002).
[378] Libby Adler. Gay Priori. Duke University Press (2018).

THE ISSUE OF NEW-AGE TOURNEYS NOT WORKING FOR QUEER LAW PROFESSIONALS

A 2010 research report by the Minority Corporate Counsel Association (MCCA) describes the troubles LGBT+ people still face in large firms. They state:

> Overall, the research found that LGBT attorneys are committed to their law firms and profession. Some expressed concerns about their opportunities for advancement and work/life balance issues. So, for many LGBT attorneys, their professional concerns are no different from their non-LGBT peers. However, some do have concerns about their firms' true commitment to diversity and inclusion and at times this impacts their ability to fully contribute at work. Also, when LGBT women and attorneys of color were asked whether they felt treated equally to their peers, they reported higher levels of disparity than their gay, white male counterparts.
>
> "MCCA's objective in examining these experiences was to craft advice and recommendations to assist law firms to foster more-inclusive and supportive environments for LGBT attorneys," said Veta Richardson.
>
> In addition, a special section of the report is dedicated to raising awareness about the challenges faced by transgender attorneys, which are quite separate and distinct from those faced by lesbian, gay and bisexual attorneys.
>
> MCCA's Sustaining Pathways report contains a number of general recommendations for law firms seeking to create more diverse and inclusive workforces. In addition to those recommendations, The New Paradigm of LGBT Inclusion suggests additional approaches to address the inclusion of LGBT attorneys in the following areas:
> - Leadership,
> - Recruitment,
> - Retention, inclusion and the work environment,
> - Professional development and advancement, and
> - Work/life balance and compensation benefits.[379]

The complete guide can be found here:

https://www.mcca.com/wp-content/uploads/2017/04/Book10-Lavender.pdf

One examination of the workplace not working for queer (and disabled) workers is the apparentness of accommodations for them. Though, studies show that this is just as the other issues in queer treatment in big law: the marginalized are left out:

> Lawyers who are racial minorities have lower odds than White LGBQ lawyers of having their accommodations granted. Longer tenure increases the odds of requesting accommodations. Working for a private organization decreases the odds; working for a large organization generally increases the odds.
>
> Conclusions: Those most needing accommodations, such as lawyers with disabilities and women, are more likely to request accommodations. Disabled lawyers, older women lawyers, older racial/ethnic minority lawyers, and LGBQ minority lawyers have relatively low odds of having requests granted. The results highlight the need to consider intersectional identities in the accommodation process.[380]

This is certainly an issue in big law.

Bias in the law against queer populations is another huge factor as to why big law may not be as receptive to queer people as we would hope. These biases are outlined by the ABA in the beginning of this paper, but again include:

- **Prevalence of subtle biases.** Almost 4 of 10 (38.5%, 1,076) of all respondents reported perceptions or experiences of subtle but unintentional biases. More than

---

[379] MCCA. New Research Report Finds LGBT Attorneys Still Experiencing a Number of Challenges in Large Law Firms. MCCA (2010).

[380] Blanck et. Al. Diversity and Inclusion in the American Legal Profession: Workplace Accommodations for Lawyers with Disabilities and Lawyers Who Identify as LGBTQ+. Springer Link (2020).

1 in 5 respondents (21.7%, 607) noted the experience of subtle and intentional biases.
- **Prevalence of mental health conditions.** One-quarter (25.0%, 830) of respondents reported a health impairment, condition or disability. Of the 1,374 total responses, almost one-third (30.8%) reported a mental condition, which could include depression, anxiety and cognitive conditions such as attention deficit hyperactivity disorder (ADHD), autism and traumatic brain injury.
- **Variations in bias and intersectional identities.** Approximately 16.6% of the lawyers responding identified as lesbian, gay or bisexual, and 0.4% identified their sexual orientation as open. Of 67 lawyers who were women and identified as LGB with a health condition, slightly more than half (52.2%, 35) reported they had experienced discrimination in their workplaces. Lawyers with a health condition or impairment and who identify as a person with a disability reported experiencing more overt forms of discrimination, such as bullying and harassment, as compared to people who do not have such conditions. Attitudinal biases and structural barriers may be even more challenging for those with multiple identities that intersect.
- **Bias mitigation strategies.** When asked to report strategies that were especially effective in lessening either overt or subtle forms of bias or discrimination in their workplaces, fewer than half (46%) reported finding effective strategies. Mentoring within (20.5%, 1,490) and outside (18.4%, 1,335) their organizations was reported as an effective mitigation strategy.
- **Requests for workplace accommodations.** More than one-quarter of all respondents (28.4%, 807) reported requesting a workplace accommodation from their organization. Of the 730 respondents who reported a health condition, impairment or disability, fewer than half (42.9%, 313) had requested an accommodation.[381]

Lawyers are also called to be "super-citizens," so their existence, whether queer or ally, can be monumental

---

[381] ABA. ABA study: Disabled, LGBTQ+ lawyers face discrimination. ABA (2020).

for other queer folks. Arkles et. al. describe the "role of lawyers in trans liberation," stating:

> Underlying much of this conflict is a question about the role of legal advocacy in empowering transgender and gender-nonconforming people who are low income and/or people of color. Broadly speaking, almost all national LGB"T" legal advocacy since its inception in the 1970s has focused on attaining "formal legal equality" in legislation and court decisions, particularly in the areas of sodomy laws and gay marriage.5 The common framing is that gay people are just like everybody else—they deserve the same rights and entitlements as straight people.6 This approach reinforces the idea that the entitlements of capitalism and democracy (such as privacy, property, independence, the pursuit of wealth, and formal marriage), as they exist in our current neoliberal economic system, are the things that we all (including gay and lesbian people) want, and that these entitlements benefit us more than any other goals we might otherwise pursue.7 Furthermore, this thinking assumes or implies that homophobia, transphobia, violence, and premature death of trans and queer8 people would be mitigated by the (hetero) normalization of gay identity within the narrative of consumerism, privacy, national security, and safety that the law embodies and protects.
>
> A legal strategy that merely extends existing rights and values to include gays, lesbians, bisexual people, and transgender people without looking at the racism, classism, ableism, homophobia, transphobia, xenophobia, and corruption that maintain capitalism will only protect the structures of empire that oppress poor people and people of color. Conversely, our analysis centers on the idea that the structures that result in decreased life chances for members of our communities, and for all people of color, poor people, trans people, queer people, and people with disabilities, are deeply rooted in and inextricably linked with the legal system as we know it. If the problems faced by our communities are rooted in and enforced by the legal system, then meaningful change would have to come from outside of it. As such, we believe in a theory of change based in mass mobilization of communities, rather than elite (strictly legal) strategies. This belief comes from an understanding that significant change for those on the bottom has never been granted from those on top. We believe that the

most significant, lasting, and sustainable way to make change is through community organizing that mobilizes those persons directly impacted. Nonetheless, we believe there are many important ways for lawyers to support social movements.

As transgender legal work continues to develop and grow, we believe it is crucial to consider what lessons we can learn from lawyer participation in other social movements. In particular, we examine the ways in which lawyers may intentionally or unintentionally consolidate power in social movements and undermine the potential for systemic change and social justice. Applying these considerations to transgender legal advocacy, we offer alternative frameworks that permit lawyers to participate in and support social movements without replicating structures of oppression. These frameworks are rooted in the creation of spaces of collaboration, with community-organizing principles at their heart.[382]

Lawyers can be placed at the heart of the queer movement, so this analysis is showing that queer folks need lawyers to be more diligent in their treatment of trans and queer of color populations.

The (now common) issue of a misfocus of resources/funds/strategies is apparent for queer people too. Leonore Carpenter details this for Penn Law, stating:

> An outside observer might expect that, with such forward progress, near-universal approval for high-profile LGBT-rights impact litigation would come from within the LGBT community. But while many in the community may be satisfied, there remains a stubborn and long-standing undercurrent of discord. LGBT activists from within and without the legal community have criticized both the methods by which LGBT impact litigators select issues to prioritize, and the priorities themselves. Critics have characterized impact litigators' prioritization methods as exclusionary and elitist, and the priorities themselves as assimilationist,

---

[382] Arkles et. al. Role of Lawyers in Trans Liberation: Building a Transformative Movement for Social Change. Seattle University School of Law (2010).

retrogressive, and unresponsive to the needs of people of color, transgender people, and the poor.[383]

Again and again, transgender people and queer people of color get left out of the prosperity of gay people (aka white gay men).

Finding the right firm can be immensely helpful for a queer lawyer. A Harvard Crimson article discusses LGBT+ lawyers' barriers in working for firms, though the writer states, "All members of the panel said that at their progressively minded law firms, discrimination in the workplace has never been a barrier to their success."[384]

Networks are also a big help. One helpful resource I found in my research was the National Center for Transgender Equality, which features a "Trans Legal Services Network Directory" and a mission that states:

> The National Center for Transgender Equality advocates to change policies and society to increase understanding and acceptance of transgender people. In the nation's capital and throughout the country, NCTE works to replace disrespect, discrimination, and violence with empathy, opportunity, and justice.[385]

Resources of such can make all the difference for a queer lawyer, especially when at a tough, large firm.

WHY THAT IS A DEEPER ISSUE FOR CULTURE

---

[383] Getting Queer Priorities Straight: How Direct Legal Services Can Democratize Issue Prioritization in the LGBT Rights Movement.
[384] Hana Rouse. Lawyers Discuss LGBT Barriers. Harvard Crimson (2010).
[385] National Center for Transgender Equality. NCTE Website. NCTE (2021).

Representation matters. Queer lawyers in large firms matter. It is important for us to see queer lawyers in society, especially those of color and those that identify as trans or other marginalized genders/sexualities. This cannot be debated.

The deeper cultural issue of accountability and respectability are key in understanding that without the influence of queer lawyers in large law firms, that could spell disasters in terms of community for queer people and the legal field in general. A day without a queer lawyer could be a real concept. We need queer lawyers, trans lawyers, queer lawyers of color, and all the like, because it is important for the overall goals of equity, inclusion, excellence, and prosperity.

There is certainly a need, in big law and in law in general, to acknowledge more than white cisgender gay men. Kelly McNamee calls this problem out in a story/article that describes lunches with the "typical crowd" and the need for change in big law. He states:

> Discussions should call for a more accurate representation of the queer community in the legal profession, one that embraces or, at the very least, acknowledges the reality of intersectionality. Without this, efforts to improve LGBT diversity will either plateau or continue to provide a limited platform aimed to assist only those members of our community who already enjoy the perks of some real, or perceived, privilege.
>
> Private practice as a whole would benefit from these discussions. The brilliant transgender man who graduated summa cum laude from a top school, sat through 25 on-campus interviews, and failed to receive a single call back offer, would appreciate these discussions. The firm that attempted to recruit a black, gender non-conforming queer person with credentials to die for and a reluctance to even consider a position in private practice for fear of discrimination would be eager to participate in these discussions. And, I would wager, the white, privileged, gay

> men I had lunch with nearly 10 years ago, many who now sit in positions of power across the country, would welcome and seek to advance these discussions.[386]

The full story/article is quite the read.

It is also important to note that queer struggles relate to civil rights, feminism, and other progressive movements/struggles. Shannon Gilreath for the DU Law Review states this incredibly well, saying:

> Rather than abandon feminism as much of queer theory suggests, gay men—and all LGBT people—should embrace feminism as a fundamental component of an ethical movement toward substantive, social, and legal equality.[387]

The state has long been against homosexuality, feminism, progressiveness in general, so the need to band with others for a common good is a necessity for queer people in law.

Remembering to keep up this good fight is an important tenet in the queer community as well. Protests, litigation, funds, lawyers, access, and the like is all pivotal in the fight for a more equal world.

Education in the community and about the community (particularly for allies) is also key. Queer perspective/theory/thought is key in the fueling of the movement (it is, in fact, a great resource). Queer professors, queer lawyers, and queer scholars make a huge difference for those that are queer in and out of the legal field.[388]

With education and great training: we can learn to combat bias against queer folx as best we can. Screening

---

[386] Kelly McNamee. Other Than Gay. NYSBA Journal (2021).
[387] Shannon Gilreath. Feminism and Gay Liberation. Denver University Law Review (2013).
[388] Brookes & Parkes. Queering Legal Education. The University of British Columbia Law (2004).

for bias in firms and on juries and with clients and fighting discrimination head on and other forms of simply "fighting the status quo" are everyday wins for the queer community.

As James Leipold outlines:

> As LGBT lawyers have stood and been counted--as a once invisible part of the bar has been revealed as a measurable demographic--the opportunities for LGBT lawyers and the support they find in the workplace have both increased dramatically.[389]

This fight must be kept on. As Neil Kelly brilliantly puts it: "THE TIME TO ADDRESS DIVERSITY AND INCLUSION IS NOW!"[390]

Humanizing queer folk (especially trans and queer folx of color) is so important. The *Bostock c*ase is reminiscent of why:

> No matter what the decision might augur for the Roberts Court, it remains true that an employer who fires a person for being gay or transgender violates Title VII of the Civil Rights Act.
>
> For transgender Americans, *Bostock* means even more than what it says: the decision humanizes us in a setting where we are only rarely seen.[391]

We, as queer folx, need to be seen, heard, and loved for who we are.

---

[389] James Leipold. Stand and Be Recognized. Southwestern Law Review (2013).
[390] Neil Kelly. The Time to Address Diversity and Inclusion is Now. Houston Lawyer (2017).
[391] Rachel Seploi. Bostock's Inclusive Queer Frame. Virginia Law Review (2021).

So, does this system of large law firms and law in general significantly fail for queer and undoubtedly other numerous and important population(s)?

Perhaps, but perhaps it's like elite universities where diversity is really tough and often takes a backseat to "performance," "comfort-ability," and all the like. Perhaps queer people have made gains, but the most marginalized queer communities (trans and queer folks of color) are still largely not helped to the same degree as some other "more privileged" queer communities (which is a MAJOR WORRY and a theme in queer America and the queer world in general). The marginalized get left behind while the "privileged community" celebrates prosperity: a cruel American story.

Though, I will say, sadly, it seems like the pools of minorities (in all senses not just racially) for "the law" are similar to those for colleges: not as large as hoped; hyper-competitive to find talent; disappointing rates of retention; affected by racism, sexism, misogyny, homophobia, transphobia, income discrimination, and all the like. All those factors seem highly apparent in both. I often wonder what the solution to this all is, and it seems like better K-12 schooling for socioeconomically disadvantaged communities is a good start, but there, at the same time, needs to be big pushes for equity in the law, colleges, workplaces, and all areas in which people persist. That's what I'm hoping for studying marginalization in both the law and education now (and culture in general too).

It makes you wonder about what is truly equitable in society and what is old guard that could be changed for better but rather is not for the "better sake of all" given the "testament" of precedence as opposed to the "propositions" of the new....

Perhaps this is just another issue or conundrum of American diversity... though whether or not it is simply just another question of "what's best for the 'majority' or the 'powerful'" is also a major question to ask when one reads this work.

Perhaps the most marginalized of queer lawyers (and probably queer lawyers in general, still, to be honest) are at even more of a deficit than minorities or women in terms of their treatment in terms of the legal profession and especially big law, which is really sad. This paper seems to show that there are still a lot of issues that queer people (again, especially trans and queer folks of color) face on a day-to-day basis in large law firms: and there is still much work to be done to make for better environments for these individuals to come out, break out, and thrive in.

Again, big law firms are simply not as diverse or diversely trained as we'd hope...

Though, my general hope (and perhaps many others, like people that read this work) is that with papers of such in this field, and of course, (almost inherently—well maybe—damn—inherently) other fields too, people will fight to make "transitions" to:

A) Better Diversity Numbers in Big Law and Especially Powerful Positions in Such

B) Support/Encourage/Foster Diversity at All Turns of the Table in Big Law

C) Place an Importance on the Ethics of Diversity in Fields Such as Corporate Law   but Expanding to Perhaps All Other Fields (Thus, Law Being an Example)

CONCLUSION: "A REMINDER OF WHY LAW IS THE LEAST DIVERSE FIELD IN THE U.S."

Could contentiousness in the law be a bigger deterrent than we thought?

Queer lawyers, and especially "marginalized queer lawyers" face a ton. This has to be looked into more so as an example of a calling for diversity, equity, and inclusion in big law. It is simply imperative at this point in queer progress. 2010 and 2015 came: 2021 is another time for queer progress: though in more progressive fields now (not just marriage and other hot-button issues).

I wonder if the cutthroat/argumentative/strenuous nature of law (in this case, especially as it pertains to large law firms) is proceeding toward a future where we continue to see few minorities (in the general sense here not just ethnic minorities) as they are weeded out due to discrimination, stress, and challenges from workload, peers, professors, judges, and the like? Or will we see a push for difference? Gen Z is more queer than recent generations... will that aide in the process?

Is the former really where we're going in law............? Or the latter?

This "just" field? With all its "just" people? Where is it headed in terms of diversity?

Right.... well as I said in another paper: "this is America, right?"

"Hustle, hustle, hustle, hustle; Hustle, hustle, hustle, hustle; Hustle, hustle, hustle

Same old shit, just a different day; Out here tryna get it, each and every way
Mama need a house, baby need some shoes; Times are getting hard, guess what I'ma do

Hustle, hustle, hustle, hard; Hustle, hustle, hustle, hard; Hustle, hustle, hustle, hard
Closed mouths don't get fed on this boulevard

Big bank in my pocket; Double up with my profit
See this shit then I cop it; Gimme that there and then drop it

Homie, hold up with my mojo; Peep the whip and the logo
Twenty fours and they low pro; I bet she fucking, I know so

Nigga ain't no doubt about it; Riding 'round with that rocket
Load it up and I cock it; Send 'bout a couple off in your noggin'

Hear them eight o eights and they knocking; Whole club and they rocking
Rose in them buckets; All my homies up in here vibing

Nigga big shit in my household; Real niggas I die for
Creeping off in that Tahoe; All about their Delogione

Nigga don't stop the party; We be getting naughty
Old kimosabe homie's; Chiefing like I'm Marley

'Cause it's the same old shit, just a different day; Out here tryna get it, each and every way
Mama need a house, baby need some shoes; Times are getting hard, guess what I'ma do

Hustle, hustle, hustle, hard; Hustle, hustle, hustle, hard; Hustle, hustle, hustle, hard
Closed mouths don't get fed on this boulevard"

-- Ace Hood

"The 'America' Problem"

TABLE OF CONTENTS

INTRODUCTION: "AMERICA IS WILD, FOR REAL"

BRIEF AMERICAN HISTORY OF THE MARGINALIZED

BRIEF ANALYSIS OF WHITE SUPREMACY TODAY

THE ISSUE OF WHITE AS THE "NORM"

THE PROBLEM OF AMERICAN CULTURE

THE PROBLEM OF AMERICA

CONCLUSION: "AMERICA TO ME"

> "You make me want to throw my pager out the window
> Tell mci to cut the phone calls
> Break my lease so I can move
> 'cause you a bug a boo, a bug a boo
> I want to put your number on the call block
> Have aol make my e-mails stop
> 'cause you a bug a boo
> You buggin what? you buggin who? you buggin me!
> And don't you see it ain't cool"
>
> -- Destiny's Child

INTRODUCTION: "AMERICA IS WILD, FOR REAL"

America is a wild place: just look at Florida (sorry, bad joke). But seriously, this nation where:

- 60% of people are purely white (76% mostly white)
- 49% is male
- Mixed race people are 3% of the population
- 14% are foreign born
- 19% are LatinX
- 13% is black
- 5% is Asian
- 17% is over 65
- 22% is youth under 18
- Where there are 3 people per household on average
- Nearly 90% finish high school but only about a third earn their BA
- 9% of people under 65 are disabled though 26% of all American people are disabled
- 64% are working
- 11% are in poverty,
- 3%-10% are queer (depending upon the state--detailed in a subsequent paragraph)

What eclectic and yet white-supremacy-yielded figures.[392] As a black female educator outlines for *Diverse*, "What is fit? What does fit look like? Who determines who fits in a position or an institution? White supremacy is the answer to those questions and the root of the problem."[393] You can imagine how 76% mostly whites can lead to the troubles we have today and have had throughout the time of the states.

Queer people being significantly more populous in certain states rather than others (Alabama, Arkansas,

---

[392] US Census Bureau. US Demographics. US Government (2020). & UCLA Williams Institute. LGBT Data & Demographics. UCLA (2020).
[393] Diverse Staff. White Supremacy: Get Out the Way. Diverse (2018).

Kansas, Kentucky, Mississippi, North Dakota, South Dakota, Tennessee, and Wyoming feature around 3.5%, while D.C. has almost 10% and numerous states have around 5%--California, Massachusetts, Nevada, New Hampshire, New York, Oregon, Vermont, and Washington)[394] is another big showing of the heteronormative, oppressive, patriarchy we live in.

This creates problems of the law in oh so many ways.

BRIEF AMERICAN HISTORY OF THE MARGINALIZED

Pick up one of many texts that outline American history from the losers' point of view (*A People's History of the US, Born Losers, Like People in History, Simple Justice, The Black Butterfly*, etc.) and you will find a myriad of reasons as to why America as a culture is truly problematic. A country designed for able-bodied, straight, male whites; stolen viciously from Natives; built on the backs of blacks; and kept together by LatinX workers. To think that this isn't evident in American culture even still today, is a joke.

Ethnic intimidation and discrimination are very real.[395] This country was first and foremost a racist nation; there is little debate left about that despite conservative rhetoric. The issue persists through facets like education,

---

[394] UCLA School of Law. Adult LGBT Population in the United States. UCLA (2020).
[395] 4 Summ. Pa. Jur. 2d Criminal Law § 9:63 Ethnic Intimidation Defined. 2 (2021). 29C Ohio Jur. 3d Criminal Law: Substantive Principles/Offenses § 1515 Ethnic Intimidation. 3 (2021). & Bill Quigley. Racial Discrimination and the Legal System: The Recent Lessons of Louisiana. United Nations (2021).

immigration, criminality, employment, discrimination, harassment, corporate, social, and other issues.[396]

Race is indeed a big issue in this country and will persist until things change on a significant basis, most of the tough work being needed to be done by white, straight, able, and cis-gendered folks (particularly men). This is another non-debatable fact.[397]

BRIEF ANALYSIS OF WHITE SUPREMACY TODAY

White supremacy today is arguably and probably the biggest threat to this nation that we face today. I don't care to entertain this topic, but it is far-reaching, problematic, and an American issue that needs to be improved upon. The ADL outlines this issue stating:

> Among domestic extremist movements active in the United States, white supremacists are by far the most violent, committing about 83% of the extremist-related murders in the United States in the past 10 years and being involved in about 52% of the shootouts between extremists and police. White supremacists also regularly engage in a variety of terrorist plots, acts and conspiracies. However, white supremacists also have a high degree of involvement with traditional forms of criminal activity as well as ideologically-based criminal activity. Most of the murders committed by white supremacists are done for non-ideological reasons. However, even if such murders are ignored, white supremacists still

---

[396] John Friedl. MAKING A COMPELLING CASE FOR DIVERSITY IN COLLEGE ADMISSIONS. University of Pittsburgh Law Review (1999). & Michael Kaufman. READING, WRITING, AND RACE: THE CONSTITUTIONALITY OF EDUCATIONAL STRATEGIES DESIGNED TO TEACH RACIAL LITERACY. University of Richmond Law Review (2007). & William Van Alstyne. AFFIRMATIVE ACTIONS. Wayne Law Review (2000).
[397] Information from study as a Higher Education scholar at UW.

commit the most lethal violence of any domestic extremist movement in the United States.

Watching the US the last 3 years (2019-2021) has been insane, and I think it's tough to equate the amount of racist behavior that goes on in this country (I've seen way, way too many videos of wild ass people acting wild as hell to deviate from that view of this country). We need to be better in terms of race in America today, people of the United States.[398]

White supremacy affects everyone and must be fought throughout these 2020's that look promising as a vessel, but the waters look treacherous. We must be aware and woke to take on the ocean of hate that surrounds us in these states.

THE ISSUE OF WHITE AS THE "NORM"

Whiteness as the normal and white normativity are a plague on this nation. The lack of acknowledgment of people of color is atrocious in this country. Whiteness as the "norm" benefits few save white people, and even then, it is a question of whether white people should truly see themselves as the "norm," given their oppressiveness and history of doing people wrong. As "The Anti-Racist Educator" explains:

> Rather than an identity, "whiteness" is a racial discourse that privileges white people and that asserts white people as the norm (Leonardo, 2002).
>
> Whiteness is reflected in the people's thoughts, actions and in the functions, outcomes of institutions and systems. This means that white people can disassociate from whiteness when

---

[398] Information from experience as a race scholar in America circa 2019-2021.

they commit to anti-racism. Similarly, people of colour can aspire to, and endorse, whiteness when their thoughts and actions privilege white people – whether it is conscious or not.

According to Bhopal, understandings of whiteness stem from processes of structural racism which work to disadvantage people of colour and advantage white people. Whiteness is not an individual identity, it is one that is embedded in institutions as being the predominant identity. In such white spaces, whiteness and white Western practices are the norm and those which do not comply with these are seen as outsiders and other.[399]

Whiteness as the normal is problematic because it holds minorities back and only empowers white people. The show, The Bachelor, with its treatment of minorities is a great example of "typical white America making whiteness the one and only standard of greatness."[400]

White normativity, or the on-goings of whiteness are also problematic because they push all other cultures to the side for the sake of the benefit of whiteness and white people. A white male that has a criminal record is about as likely to get a job as an educated and non-criminal-past black person simply due to racist biases.[401]

Yeah, this is a problem, and one perhaps the law can (often) weigh in upon and should, though the law is troubled too and falls incredibly short of this objective (read other governmental-inclined papers in this thesis).

---

[399] The Anti-Racist Educator. Whiteness. The Anti-Racist Educator (2021).
[400] Eric Deggans. Dismantling 'The Bachelor's' Racist And Sexist Elements Has Only Just Begun. NPR (2020).

[401] This is found in many sociological, criminological, and psychological references, but here is one: Pager et. al. Sequencing Disadvantage. Harvard University (2009).

THE PROBLEM OF AMERICAN CULTURE

American culture is nationalistic, backwards often, oppressive, appropriating, problematic, and a disaster all at once. Are there good and even great aspects? Certainly, but to be an American is to, in effect, know that America is problematized and often needs changes (why do you think we trade the Democrats and Republicans every few years; we need change).

Since 2020 and onward, I think it is high time Americans imagined a "New America," one that is tolerant, diverse, (still) powerful, united, and awesome.

What will it take for us to get there? How can we, as an American people, accomplish this objective?

THE PROBLEM OF AMERICA

America as an establishment can often be a major problem of the law.

America has a myriad of tough issues that percolate and permeate throughout our entire society: hoping for a better America is not a hope, but indeed a fight.

The books I outline in the other paper for this course ("The 'Race' Problem") discusses four major works (*The Color of Law, Supreme Inequality, In the Interests of Justice,* and *The New Jim Crow*) that all outline this very relevant problem of inequality that draws upon racial, gendered, sexualized, abled motives.

The effect of these motives is enormously powerful and are often the reasons why minorities and other marginalized groups have such a difficult time making it in this "equal and free" country (eye roll).

CONCLUSION: "AMERICA TO ME"

I am a black, queer, disabled male American. I am enlisted in this "fight against the Man," so, America, to me, is more problematized than I can even imagine or know. That's simple facts. I'm in this fight to make America less problematized, but still the waters are treacherous.

"Everybody plays the fool
There's no point in wondering why people do what they do
It's alright to be confused
But don't lose sight of the truth
Girl, it's him, it's not you
So what if he don't call when he's supposed to
So what if he don't care
So what if when you cry, he don't hold you
You don't need him to be there
So what if when you're mad he says you're crazy
You just make him insecure
No, you didn't lose the girl you used to be
You just let yourself get a little hurt
But so what

> So what; So what
> It happens to the best of us
> So what; So what; So what
> It happens to the best of us"
>
> -- Louis the Child

CONCLUSION
28. Conclusive Capstone Paper – "MLS Feelings – An Advocate of the Advocates"
29. A Law School Experiment – "No Accommodations is AKA Pain"
30. "Conclusion to LSAT I – The Pain of Studying Marginalization"
31. "Another Year of More Damages" – A Concluding Poem
32. "Still & Still" – A 2nd Concluding Poem
33. "A CALL TO LAWYERS – FIX THESE ISSUES" -- A Final Paper

"MLS Feelings – An Advocate of the Advocates"

TABLE OF CONTENTS

INTRODUCTION: "EVERY PART OF ME IS BEAUTIFUL"
MY LAW-DRIVEN LIFE
MY LAW SCHOOL EXPERIENCE
THE DIFFERENCE THE LAW CAN MAKE
WHY THE LAW MATTERS TO ME
BUT, HOW I ACTUALLY FEEL ABOUT THE LAW

THE PLACE OF THIS THESIS IN THE LEGAL REALM: "THE CALLING OF FUTURE LAWYERS AND LAW BUFFS"
THE PAIN OF THE LEGAL SYSTEM
THE "ONE YEAR SPRINT" OF LAW SCHOOL: "CONFESSIONS OF AN MLS"
WHY I WROTE THIS THESIS: "THE MIDDLE GROUND OF AN MLS"
CONCLUSION: "AN ADVOCATE OF THE ADVOCATES"

> "Why did they envy? Why you go against me? When I got trendy, why you ain't commend me? Why when I needed it, why you couldn't lend me? Why you was secretive, frontin' like you friendly? Why did you fear that, held my career back? Kick it like air max, I don't wanna hear that; 'Cause now I see-see-see-see all your run-down; Niggas better have my money by sun down"
> -- Nicki Minaj

INTRODUCTION: "EVERY PART OF ME IS BEAUTIFUL"

I've been blessed with a beautiful soul. I'm smart, funny, pretty, and just a bit crazy (so it's fun). I say that to say that I've also been blessed to be able to develop in multiple humanistic fields, all of which have developed me into a true "people person". I know culture well, as I do higher education, and now law and hopefully business in the future. Combining these fields allows me a certain insight that I think is truly wonderous and not quite found in too many people. I feel confident that each part of me will help me to better the world in the ways I can and hope to, and I know that each part of me is beautiful because of that. These masterful strokes of the paintbrush are leading towards a Mona Lisa that I know will have an impact on the world, and it all makes me feel so blessed. The law, now, is another beautiful part of me.[1]

MY LAW-DRIVEN LIFE

The law has always been a major driver of my life, and now that I have a legal degree it all makes sense. It's funny, I look back on my life and I was perhaps in "mini-lawyer training" starting from perhaps the end of elementary school. My dad was a lawyer and so for me to be the rebel I was I needed to be one of sorts too (gotta know the system to fight the system). What's funny now is that I realize the world is run by the law, so I think of study of the legal system as necessary to being a rebel now, especially given the current climate of the US. The law has always been something that has been helping (or sometimes hurting) me, but it was *always* best that I *knew* it, because I did, would, and still do *need* it.[2]

To this day I still debate going into law further, but I'm unsure. I'm still trying to figure how I can best impact people in my life to truly maintain true to self and the goals presented by my life. The law is a field that I know is more powerful than most, but I'd hate to lose myself to the thinking/writing/mannerisms of lawyers, which isn't quite my demeanor or purpose. I see myself more as an influential writer and future-political-type, but my life (with going on 3-4 degrees, multiple cities resided in [including many major West Coast places], tons of friends in a number of places and placings, and a writing track record that would liken me to a star) is kinda crazy and I'm still trying to figure it all out. I have yet to find where I fit in. Though, I know a knowledge (and a degree) in the law is worthwhile in more ways than one. I am proud to say that I've been to and through law school (though, gladly, am not a lawyer), and proud that I can say that I have mastered the law. [3]

My thesis, I think, is a great example for the people that are working towards change for the betterment of this country, and I hope that this work serves as a good resource for the people protesting and fighting for the wellbeing of others. I am thrilled at the idea that this work could be considered a starting point for many groups that are trying to subvert the oppressive systems that persist to enlist sexism, racism, homophobia, transphobia, and discrimination of all sorts. I often think that creating resources of such in fields such as this is beneficial for lots of people. GRE and even WPDC (GRE being my education graduate school thesis and WPDC being my undergraduate thesis in American Studies & Ethnicity) were guides into various marginalization and drug topics that I think really helped people understand some concepts that I enjoy and am able to communicate on so that others can learn what I've learned.[4] This thesis is no different. It's quite the exhausting cycle for me to write these resource guides for others while studying in various programs, to be honest, but I think it's been great to be able to write these works for the betterment of society.

MY LAW SCHOOL EXPERIENCE

My law school experience was wild. I managed to fight through some challenging grades (two midterms with D grades were a harsh entry), learned to think like a lawyer, wrote my thesis with confidence, and truly learned the law (or at least some of it – *Corporate and Social Law*). Being a Corporate/Social law student was interesting and very empowering, especially considering the fact that I have now been to law school. Just saying that makes me happy and I think able to do things I wouldn't be able to if that statement weren't a fact. I think the learning aspect of truly "logicalizing" arguments that are viable and strong is a skill many students and people would benefit from a ton.[5]

One professor told me that she thought it was really cool that I was studying the law in this sense and expressed to me that she wished more people would take just a year of law school (and we both thought this would be a benefit to society).[6] It's weird to think of how much power the law holds, and how some people are significantly unaware of legal notions. I wish that legal studies were more a part of the norm, I even wrote a law (in my Legislative Drafting class) that would allow for high school students to be able to study the law instead of economics at the end of high school (a requirement in many states), which I think is a very relevant change/addition to the curriculum we teach our youth, but I digress. Learning how to write the law in that class and so many other subtleties were great and a big step for me. Law school was not a joke and not something that was light: this study (sprint of a year) was rigorous, as is the law. [7]

Other milestones like learning about the ethics of lawyering; corporate issues, remedies, contracts, and administrative law in two "Directed Research" courses; and a full load of legal classes related to gender, education, negotiation and mediation, trusts and estates, and even big law firms the final semester to round out my Corporate/Social studies were so influential in my life and I know I will carry the knowledge this program has provided into more and more intricate work in faucets yet to be determined.[8]

As a sidenote, it's an interesting idea that if the law allowed for more people to be involved in a lucrative "lawyer-type" role, it would be a better field (Yikes! An actual solution here!). If MLS's, LLM's, paralegals,

MSLA's, and other legal professionals were allowed to be more involved in legal processes (as lawyers are still the only big fish in the pond in terms of the law), perhaps there would be more equity in the law, the legal profession, the prices for legal services, access to legal services, and many other important things that would make the law a fairer field should certainly be explored. I believe this firmly being an MLS.[9]

THE DIFFERENCE THE LAW CAN MAKE

No matter how you feel about the law or lawyers or judges or paralegals even, the law can make a difference in the life of an individual in a troubling situation, while also or at a different time making a difference in the wellbeing of society as a whole in an issue or overarching situation (think Supreme Court decisions and the like). Law has a huge impact on the world and certainly shouldn't be taken lightly by anyone, especially those looking for social change. If we, as people, can enlist lawyers for good, perhaps the world will ease into being a better and better place. The law is powerful enough for that: I promise you.[10]

WHY THE LAW MATTERS TO ME

The law matters to me because it's the biggest difference maker out there. The law is vicious, rich, helpful as fuck, and a dominate force within society. As a macro-scale person, why wouldn't law matter to me (let alone my background)? The law literally rules the world.[11]

Law changes stuff. Lawyers are powerful. Lobbyists are powerful. Judges are powerful. Lawmakers are powerful. The law certainly has its perks and upsides, much as I've given it trouble throughout this thesis. The law is the law, and no matter what this thesis says, the law will still remain the law in most senses, fortunately or not. I don't think anyone can change that: too many powerful lawyers are strapped and willing to deal with that fight.[12]

But, hopefully, over time, the law will improve with critiques such as this thesis; and that, I believe, is a remarkable part about the role people involved in the law can play (even and especially if not lawyers). One lawyer (or law person or even a nonlawyer, layperson) can truly change the world via the law.

That's why the law matters to me.

BUT, HOW I ACTUALLY FEEL ABOUT THE LAW

Even if I know that the law matters and can arguably change the world more than anything else, I still feel some typa way about the law. The law is fucked up in so many ways (notice that this work of "problems" is simply a primer, an introduction into this rabbit hole into Wonderland that is the legal system). I don't truly care to be a lawyer (at least currently) like my father was for 25 years. I don't have a desire to represent clients in an impartial way. I want to be able to be partial and a ridiculous person and on the side of righteousness (not the side of my client) and a rebel and not bound by the crazy ass rules of lawyering. I am SO, SO GLAD to be an MLS rather than a JD. A knowledge of the law is important and pivotal for my life and my pursuit of helping others, but the role of a lawyer (ie. lawyering) is not my calling at all. I simply am not my father.[13]

That is to say, I think highly of the law and its agents, but I'm also more skeptical of the system than I think most are, due to the fact that I am knowledgeable about the field in a complex and deep manner with an approach that's uncommony educated and interdisciplinary. Though, I am happy to be able to expose the issues I do throughout this thesis to a lawyer-type and non-lawyer-type of audience alike, and it's been riveting to work through the arguments and logic needed to express these conundrums of the law. Though, again, and very firmly: I am not a lawyer (at least not at this point) and do not really intend to be (at least not for quite some time). The law is a system that needs reform (in so many ways, not limited to what is in this thesis), and I'm simply doing my part to help with that, though as the role of an MLS, not a JD. This is intentional. [14]

THE PLACE OF THIS THESIS IN THE LEGAL REALM: "THE CALLING OF FUTURE LAWYERS AND LAW BUFFS"

I think this thesis will really serve to shed light on legal troubles and issues that should be addressed by the new wave of lawyers coming into and emerging in the field. Young people are needing to change the problematic things that are persisted from the past. We cannot be afraid of change as changemakers, and I really hope that the future lawyers/law buffs/even laypeople can utilize the law for good and help to make the necessary changes that we need to see in order for the law to become a more equitable, fair, and useful tool for the marginalized and, in effect, all people. [15]

The law is such a powerful system that if we let it slip away towards corporate manipulation, unfairness, injustice, and the like: we will surely be in big trouble. Rather us point out and work through the conundrums and problems of the law now (as to be proactive), rather than letting problems persist due to inaction. This thesis is truly a call to action to all people to demand and fight for reform within the legal system so that we may all benefit: Americans and citizens of the world alike. This has to be acknowledged as the chief goal of this work and the research it took to create it.[16]

THE PAIN OF THE LEGAL SYSTEM

The legal system is riddled with issues: as evidenced by the conundrums in this thesis. These issues are a social ill for marginalized people, and often the law is punitive, inaccessible, and unfair toward these groups of people that are not as well off as others. It is our duty as people fighting for social justice (if you are among us), that we understand and address these problems of the law, for the sake of those most vulnerable among us. It is no surprise that the law can solve these issues if we fight, but the fight must be brought, maintained, kept, and achieved.[17]

The pain of the legal system is massive, expansive, hurtful, immense, difficult, far-reaching, and overwhelming. But the fight is here: and it is truly ours to be had, again for the sake of those most marginalized among us.[18]

As I said in my education thesis: "We can choose to bottle it up; we can choose to run and hide; or we can choose to fight". I hope that I continue to choose to fight, the other two options don't seem like true options at all. I also hope that other people choose to see things the same way.[19]

THE "ONE YEAR SPRINT" OF LAW SCHOOL: "CONFESSIONS OF AN MLS"

I went to law school from January 2021 – December 2021: the end of the COVID Crisis. I had arrived in Denver, CO to learn at DU Sturm after a year-long sprint of education school that took the entirety (all 4 quarters) of the 2019 – 2020 year. Needless to say, education and law schools back-to-back was tough. Add in the fact that I'm a pseudo-educator (as a tutor of 10 years, but not a teacher or higher education professional at all) that studied Higher Education Leadership & Policy and a nonlawyer that studied Corporate and Social Law (two very riveting and challenging fields).[20]

Now also add in the fact that I did these degrees half in-person, half on-Zoom, and whilst writing two Master's theses that weren't attached to the schools' programs (ie. both GRE and LSAT were my own personal projects). [21]

Now continue with adding in the fact that I'm a sun-kissed Californian (and USC grad) that ventured to rainy and very grey Seattle, WA to write GRE and gain an M.Ed., and the sunny but also snowy Denver, CO to brave law school as an MLS student (not the glorious—based on how the school treated them as opposed to us MLS students—JD students).

These challenges were no match for my schizo-black-queer ass though. I rocked it throughout 2019 – 2021 (especially as a writer, let alone as a student as well), and I'm happy that law school has been a success (despite the semi-rough introduction of multiple "D" midterms), especially for the fact that I was able to write 30+ papers about the "problems of the law" while not even a JD student. I couldn't be more elated at my own personal success and am hoping this work makes a difference in the world.[22]

WHY I WROTE THIS THESIS: "THE MIDDLE GROUND OF AN MLS"

All of this is to say: I wrote this thesis because I'm in the middle ground of lawyering (being a law buff that is not a lawyer) and its problems. I am well able to label problems within the legal field while still remaining at an arms distance; a quality you would hope for in someone that is doing something of an audit of a system.[23]

The legal system is complex, and this thesis could've been approached in a variety of ways: most relating to the topic of law emphasized (environmental, social, corporate, administrative, marijuana, or whatever topics you can fancy). I chose to write to my strong suites and true passions (sociology, business, law, race, education), which led me to a Corporate/Social focus, which I must say, could be two of the most impactful sectors (these are giant sectors, both) in law. Corporations are huge and powerful, as seen in my Corporate/Administrative section papers, and social issues are imminently important for us people as social beings (and expansive as hell too). That is to say: I don't think you could pick a more pertinent lens (Corporate/Social) for current times, save for perhaps the addition of Environmental Justice.[24]

Thus, I believe that this thesis is a well-planned and well-written piece that establishes a number of issues within the current US legal structure that make it problematic for people in general, but especially those that identify as marginalized. I also believe that this thesis accomplishes the task of evaluating and calling out a multitude of problems that could be fixed by future generations of lawyers and legal professionals.[25]

And that was the purpose of this thesis; to have accomplished that to the tune of 30+ papers is enlightening and encouraging for a writer adding his sixth book to his catalogue. The major step of publishing this legal work (in legal speak and form) is a monumental achievement for me, and I know that the research will serve to better things for people that will live in the years forward.[26]

CONCLUSION: AN ADVOCATE OF THE ADVOCATES

I've learned throughout my revolutionary life that it's a lot better to try to attack the system from within and with a knowledge of the system itself, than to try and attack it as an outsider looking in with little knowledge of how the system works. I think many people understand this aspect of my approach to learning and life. I am a Corporate/Social emphasis for a reason: I want to change things from the inside and be well-equipped to help people via the system; and, I hope that other people are attempting the same thing. People that are equipped in the system and its facets are the ones that are best equipped to fight/change it. That note is more important to me than most.

I am an advocate of lawyers, troubled as they and their system are, because I believe in using the system for good. Lawyers are the way they are because they truly believe that the legal system is a better system than any other for control/order within the states, and I don't believe them to be wrong. The law system is remarkable and wonderful at many, many turns. Though, I hope that I, throughout this thesis, have been able to show evidence that the law system is certainly not perfect, and that there are, indeed, many, many instances where there is a definitive "problem" with the law.

Solving the problems established in this thesis will certainly be a mark of greatness if the numerous (a plethora, truly) issues can be handled. I only serve to highlight these issues in this work: the real work is left to the advocates.

"I'm me, don't you like what you see? Won't you get like me?
'Cause you thought that I would die; But I'm fine
I'm me, don't you like what you see? Won't you get like me?
'Cause you thought that I would die
But I'm fine (fine, fine, fine, fine)"
-- Nicki Minaj

A Law School Experiment -- "No Accommodations is AKA Pain"

> "Been through some crazy shit,
> Still kept myself sane...
> You ever been dyin' of thirst..
> And felt rain?
> You ever been told to go to hell..
> And felt flames?"
> -- Fabolous

I have accommodations in school. Usually, I get some combination of typed exams, disability related excused absence, and perhaps one or two other things.

I have gone with and without accommodations, or some form of in-between, but I was always interested in the "me now" form and how that would be impacted by not receiving accommodations in school or the workplace.

So, I tried it. It was my last semester at DU Sturm, so I thought I'd try to go without accommodations and see the result, which was shockingly interesting.

Let me preface this by saying I am very able, with a few notable quirks, though I do struggle on many days due to my schizophrenia and anxiety. I often don't want to be in class. This was not truly an option in this setting I designed. I also would have to make sure to not have too many issues.

I started the semester with 16 units out of a needed 12 to graduate (giving myself room to fail). I had 7 courses but 1 was online and 2 were weekend courses (3-hours each though) I would attend once every 2 weeks. It was a pressing schedule. Here is the list of courses with corresponding unit counts:

    Constitutional Law (Directed Research) (1)
    Advanced Legal Research (1)
    Leadership for Women in Law (Online) (2)
    Big Law, The Practice of Large Firms (2)
    Education Law (3)
    Negotiation & Mediation (3)
    Trusts & Estates (4)

So, I worked through this schedule for 6 weeks and had few issues save exhaustion from not being able to miss courses even if not feeling very well. Though, I took my Trusts & Estates midterm without "typed exams" accommodations and totally got a D due to lack of true interest in the course, the knowledge that I could in fact drop the course (which was a ton), and my horrible handwriting (no typed exams).

So, I ended up dropping Trusts & Estates, which was amazing.

I ended up doing pretty well during the semester; I was able to be in a position to get an A in most all of my courses. Though, the lack of disability related absences made things quite awful as the semester wore on. I felt as though I "had" to attend course even if I was feeling terrible and on the verge of tears, or supremely anxious, or simply down and out in any way (which happens often as a schizophrenic and anxious person).

I think the sunshine and pleasant weather helped a ton with this experiment, as was the time back in actual classrooms (after plenty of time at Zoom U), and the general fact that it was my final semester of law school. I did extremely well in the final semester, but I worry that it came at such a high cost. My mental health is certainly not in the shape in which I'd hope and I hate to regret to think that I have damaged myself in certain ways by not allowing myself the time to heal throughout the weeks as I usually do and truly need.

I told one professor, the lack of accommodations this semester was AKA pain, which it was.

In that thread, I would like to offer the insights of a group of disabled folx who were featured in a 2009 work called: *Lawyers, Lead On: Lawyers with Disabilities Share Their Insights*. Their wisdom of issues (good and bad) in various settings of being disabled follows:

General Issues
- Underrepresentation
- Issues with Disclosure & "Being Out as Disabled"
- Limited Professional Opportunities
- Hiring, Retention, Promotions, etc.
- Disability as Diverse
- The Importance of Disabled as a Minority Group

- Power of Inclusion & Importance of Peers & Community[27]

Transitioning into Law School
- The Ideas of Isolation & Combatting
- Accommodations Struggles Being Huge for Disabled Populations
- The Importance of Similar Experiences before Law School
- The Importance of Patience, Poise, & Professionalism
- Ask for What You Need & Help People Understand Importance
- Not Concentrating on Grades & Not Having to Practice as a Lawyer
- The Importance of Finding Your Advocacy
- Gender & Racial Biases on Top of Disability Biases
- The Plummeting Self Esteem of Law Students
- Depression Problems Being Common in Law School
- The Trauma of Having to Perform Well or Not Performing Well
- The Importance of Finding Self & Helping Others
- The Importance of a "I Can Succeed" Mentality
- The Importance of Disregarding Ignorance
- The Importance of Knowing You are Not Alone
- The Knowledge that Challenges are Problems to Solve
- "Limitingness" is Mitigated by Education
- Study Hard & Find Alternative Ways to Accomplish Things
- Find Things that Help You (Tech, Friends, Professors, etc.)
- Seek Support from Others & Help Others Too
- Remember Challenges Will Remain
- Trust & Train Yourself

- The Importance of Experiences & Enjoying/Living Them
- The Importance of Doing your Homework on Disability Accommodations
- The Importance of Independence
- Be Determined to Make a Difference
- The Importance of Being a Positive Example
- The Knowledge that Lawyers Change Lives
- The Knowledge that Law School is No Easy Feat
- The Knowledge that Everyone has Troubles in Law School
- Take Challenges One Step at a Time
- Go with What has Made You Successful in the Past
- Gain Knowledge & Abilities with Diverse Experiences
- Understanding that Work Opportunities are Great
- Stay in Touch with Contacts & Try to Develop Strong Relationships
- Try to Do Non-Law Stuff to Stay Balanced
- Don't be Afraid to Take Risks[28]

Disclosing Disabilities in Law
- The Importance of Disclosing Invisible Disabilities for the Sake of the Community
- Your Disability is a Part of Who You Are
- Telling Others about Your Disability Can Be Freeing
- The Importance of Finding Your Identity
- Disclosing Your Disability Can Be Crucial
- The Importance of "Somebody Like Us"
- Learn How & When to Talk about Your Disability
- The Fact that Being Out can Help a Ton
- Work Hard at Being Comfortable Being You
- Surround Yourself with People who Believe in You

- Seek out Mentors Who Appreciate Your Gifts
- Be Proud of Your Disability
- The Importance of Circumstances of Disability
- The Importance of Problems with Disclosing Disability
- Importance of "Reasonable Accommodations"
- The Importance of Knowing Your Disability, Strengths, & Weaknesses
- Get the Support You Need
- The Fact that You Can Be a Successful Lawyer even if Disabled
- The Importance of Finding Good Healthcare Providers
- Embrace Diversity & Treatment
- Medication Can Be a Savior
- Don't Be Ashamed to Ask for Help
- Don't Get Bogged Down by the Stats; Use Them!
- Do What Makes You Happy and the Rest Will Follow
- Give Things Your All
- Your Future is Up to You
- Being a Disabled Lawyer is Extraordinarily Tough
- Disclose, Discuss, Dispel if That's You
- Hang with A Good Crowd
- Stress Competence Despite Your Disability
- Be Prepared for People's Response to Your Disability
- Change the Status Quo
- Learn about Your Disability & Others'
- Disclosing Disability Takes Vulnerability, But Isn't Bad
- Make Things Work for You
- Stay Strong; You Are Who You Are[29]

Disability Identity in Law
- The Knowledge that No One is "Lesser Than" Idea

- Trust Your (Informed) Instincts
- Keep Things in Perspective
- Find "Reality Checks" Along the Way
- Don't Get Run Over by Intersectionality Issues
- Ask About Other Factors (Race, Gender, Disability, Income Status, etc.)
- The Knowledge that Tech is an Opportunity & a Challenge
- Work with Your Mentors
- Tell Your Own Story
- Gain Control of Your Reality
- The Importance of Overcoming Negativity
- The Value of Human Rights Movement
- Believe in Yourself
- Work Where You're Interested/Valued/Wanted
- Tune out Naysayers
- Push Through to Accomplishments
- Pace Yourself & Keep the Target in Mind
- Prepare for the Responses/Actions of Others
- Find Supportive People in Your Journeys
- You Can Deal with the Things You Go Through
- Lawyers Exude Influence
- Embracing Disability Can Be Very Beneficial
- Find a Sense of Vision & Purpose
- There May Be No Guide for You
- Network with the Disabled Community
- The Importance of Facing Disability
- The Importance of Intersectionality
- People Won't Always Be Tolerant
- Enable Community & Diversity
- Treat People Well
- The Importance of Strong Women
- Seek Support & Role Models
- Find & Help/Get Help from Others Similar to You
- Take Responsibility for You

- Trust Friends & Mentors
- Don't Be Intimidated
- Don't Settle for "No"
- The Importance of Achieving Results with Diplomacy
- We Are All Human
- Disabled People Can Achieve
- Disability Limits You, But Doesn't Have to Play a Major Role in Your Life
- Focus on Your Talents & Abilities, not Your Disability
- Your Disability Should Only Enhance Your Experience
- "Invisible Disabilities" Are Important Too
- Choose the Road Less Traveled
- Don't Accept "Can't"; Use It as A Motivator for You
- Find How Your Disability Advantages You
- Own Being You[30]

Career Foundations as a Disabled Person
- Find Help from the Pros
- Others Can't Always See or Acknowledge Your Disability
- Disabilities Make You Seem More "Seasoned"
- Live for Reason & Hope
- Be Intentional About Your Life Pursuits
- Disclosing Disability Can Be Complex
- Don't Be Afraid to Lead
- Believe that You Are Able
- Follow Your Heart & Find Success for You
- Enjoy the Work You Do
- Hold Fast to Your Skills & Traits
- Keep Learning
- Persevere & Live a Good Life
- The Importance of Keeping Family & Friends
- Have Fun!
- Some People will Understand You; Others Won't

- Happiness is Directly Related to Defining Yourself
- Be Realistic in Your Expectations
- Stay Humble
- Be Up for the Challenge!
- We May Be Very Different
- Try Different Things
- Be Happy in Being Fortunate
- We Can Be Blessed & Cursed
- Be A Bit Outrageous
- Love Diversity
- Share Your Prosperity
- Stand Out Well!
- Hard Work is the Key to Success
- Your Disability Should Shape You, Not Define You
- Plan Efficiently
- Have a Good Support System
- Do More, Talk Less
- Attitude is Everything
- Work Hard
- Believe that You Can Be Who You Want to Be
- Disability Can Shape You
- Success Comes from Work
- Disability Doesn't Exclude Great Contributions to Society
- Focus on What You Can Do, Not What You Can't Do
- Carry On![31]

Building Disability Awareness in Law
- Law Has an Ableism Problem
- Discrimination Based on Ability Happens
- Accommodations are not Guaranteed
- The Lack of Awareness Can Be Isolating/Harmful
- We, as Disabled Folx, Must Combat This
- Accommodations Can Help a Lot
- There Are Ways to Realize Your Dreams
- Be a Good Lawyer & Fight Stereotypes

- Don't Let Disability Define You
- Be Active in the Fight for Change
- Low Disability Numbers Can Be Startling
- What's Good for Your Career Can Often Be Bad for Your Health
- Validation is Tough in the industry
- Law Can Be Lonely (Many Minority Numbers Are Low)
- Law is Certainly not "Barrier-Free"
- Being A Good Example Makes a Difference
- Disabled Lawyers Make a Big Impact on the Field
- Law Takes Passion, Foresight, & Preparation
- We Know Ourselves & Our Needs
- Use the Tools to Succeed
- Don't Be Too Bitter about Experiences
- Don't Push Yourself Too Much
- Don't Be Too Afraid to Ask for Help
- Do Some Soul Searching
- Work Hard & Enjoy the Journey
- Being Disabled Doesn't Make You Less Qualified
- Lawyers with Disabilities Are Blazing Trails
- You'll Make Mistakes; It's OK
- Have a Positive Attitude

Reflections on the Disability Rights Movement
- Diversity is Expanding, but There is Still Much Work Ahead
- The Importance of Formal Opportunities
- Don't Assume Access will be Provided
- Access is Still very much an Issue
- Take Initiative, Others may not Know How to Act
- Find Satisfaction in Work
- Work Hard, Be Honest, & Don't Be Afraid to Ask Questions
- Don't Allow Disrespect to Destroy You
- Embrace Positive Thinking

- Be Excellent
- Others will not be Like You Oftentimes, Which Makes Things Lonely
- Own Your Own Life
- The Importance of the Breadth of Perspectives
- Apply Yourself (In Education & Experience)
- Lead!
- Disability Advocacy Brings People Better Lives
- Stay Connected in the Movement
- Find Brothers & Sisters in Disability
- Treat Others How You'd Want to Be Treated
- Discrimination is Not Uncommon; Fight It
- Help Others[32]

With all this knowledge, I think it is also important to note (going from an article my dad sent me during the end of the year) that you are what you think you are, literally.

As James Allen describes in "As A Man Thinketh," "the thinkers are the makers of themselves." You literally are what you think you are. If you think you are going to find happiness and enlightenment and heaven and whatever else, you likely will. Allen describes character as a sum of thoughts, good and bad, with an emphasis on growth of thoughts and thought processes.[33]

He describes [wo]man's mind as a garden and the fact that thoughts bear fruits and vegetables and ultimately make us the garden of wealth or lack thereof that we might eventually become due to the process of our cultivation and use. He relates that man is a "causer of [their] circumstances," and that happy and good thoughts build the body and mind up to better things.[34]

He says, "protect your mind" as it is linked to your purpose, being, and impact. The search for one's knowledge and visions of one's heart is importance and should not be taken lightly.[35]

Ultimately, we are the makers of our own futures, disabled or not.

"I wasn't from their hood, so the Westside niggas ain't really have no reason to respect a nigga
And since I went to school with them motherfuckers
Niggas from my hood actin' like they ain't accept a nigga
All that I could do was lash out
Get a couple down niggas, put the mask on, cash out
Broad day with the strap out
Can't forget it, don't regret it, gave a nigga somethin' to rap about
All that I could do was lash out
Get a couple down niggas, put the mask on, cash out
Broad day with the strap out
Last real nigga standing, I'm the one you niggas rap about
Yeah"
-- Freddie Gibbs

"Conclusion to LSAT I – The Pain of Studying Marginalization"

"Uh, name another bitch rock shit like this
Couple rap bitches try to jock my shit
Switch a flow up, they can catch this drip
Make a bitch take note when I pop my shit
Ain't met a nigga worth chasing yet
If I'm in yo' city, I made a check
Boy eat this pussy like he a vet'
His name in my phone under "Crazy Neck""
-- Renni Rucci

Law school was hard for me, but I think I did well. This thesis, I believe, is one of my best works ever, rivaled only by perhaps my first blog itself. I'm really intrigued by the ramifications of solving the problems of the law that I outline in this work, though that is mostly for others to fight for, I believe. It is truly my hope that people use this book as a way to bring up, discuss, fight against, and change these "problems of the law". If people are more equipped to do so with the help of this work: then I've done my job as a legal writer.

It's been a tough road writing GRE and LSAT back-to-back and in the COVID bubble (I'm in both the Class of 2020 and the Class of 2021 though for my efforts, finishing this program with my third degree). It has been terribly painful to study the things that marginalize people, and this research was not very different than the educational marginalizations I studied at UW or even the drug/race issues I studied at USC. Though, there are so many problems in our country today in this modernized world that it is tough to sit down and evaluate any of them for sake of brevity, pain, or any of the hinderances and anxieties we face as a society in the world of the cell phone. Though, this work of fighting to better society has to be done, especially in the cultural (and yes, legal too) realm: people truly need it currently.

The pain of studying all this marginalization and issues of equity, though, is in no comparison to the joy it brings me to know that I am writing a resource that could be used to solve the very problems the work identifies. This work was not written to be ignored; rather, it was written to be felt in an empathetic and emotional way that would inspire lawyers and nonlawyers alike to address societal issues in the present and continue to fight for the rights of those that are most at risk of those rights being violated, imposed upon, ignored, or generally wronged. I would hope that this work would serve to empower those fighting for the have-nots despite the nature of my Corporate/Social tag. I truly am looking to change these issues from the inside, and that takes a degree of knowing the Sith. But this work being used for good, for people's betterment, for societal peace, for empowerment of those that feel powerless, that's the goal. The idea of this work being utilized becoming a reality (or even just the chance of it, really) empowers me. I hope this work empowers you too.

> "You got me wrong
> You be sittin' by the bar when it's your song
> You can act like you don't like it but you do
> You do, you do, do, do, do, do (Holiday Season, nigga)
> I think I'm gonna kill the motherfuckin' DJ
> If he don't pull up, let the record replay
> Record replay, record replay
> I think I'm gonna kill the motherfuckin' DJ (yo)"
> -- Nicki Minaj

"Another Year of More Damages" – A Concluding Poem

> "Even in ya own hood,
> Bitch you ain't safe"
> -- Kash Doll

Another year,
More losses,
More wins,

Tryin' stay glad in it
As the Lord says
But it's hard, man
Social justice might be damned,
But I am as I am

The sadness in the system
Few truly believe
But what other solutions…
Are truly, true to be?

Another year of more damages,
For me

But I trudge on,
Willingly,

Another year of more damages,
For we thee,

"I should be cryin but I just can't let it show,
I should be cryin but I can't stop thinkin…
All the things you should've said,
That you never said..
All the things you should've done,
That you never did
All that said, I don't know what I should be thinkin..
Oh, darlin"
-- Tank

"Still & Still"

"You can accomplish anything,
If you survive blackness"
-- Lupe Fiasco

Heart's broken,
Even if the storm is calmed,
Like damn,
Where did we.....
You know.. Go wrong?

I've written sad song after sad song… after sad song,
Is this what I'm destined for?
A sad song bird,
Singing along...

To the pain, of each song.

Where did we...
Where did we go wrong?

Still and still,
I sing, and trudge, along.....
On and on...
Where did... we go wrong?

"Le futur c'est maintenant
Ain't nobody gonna stop me!
Don't you let the music stop now
You're more than just anybody!
Don't give up the future starts now!
We'll worry 'bout it in the mornin'
Take it to another level
You're more than just anybody
Don't give up the future starts now!"
-- Kim Petras

"A CALL TO LAWYERS – FIX THESE ISSUES"

"Same feelin' as Pac' when he got with Death Row,
Let's go!"
-- Dave East

**I laid out at least 30-50 problems the law could fix. A measly MLS student, not even a JD or even practicing attorney, law professional, or judge.
Think of the power of a plethora of lawyers to actually change these issues (and more).**

"Self love is the best love,
You made it,
Ooh yeah yeah!"
-- Teyana Taylor

"A life has no importance other than the impact it has on other lives"
-- Jackie Robinson

"You do what you can"
-- Huey Freeman

"If it helps, put the blame on me,
Have your friends come and hate on me…
But, just because I carry it well,
Doesn't make it not heavy,
It's heavy"
-- Witt Lowry & Josh Golden

LSAT I Pt. II – Le Problemes Complexe

My thesis was originally meant to be 42 papers, though came out to be 34. That is because 1) I added a couple conclusion and intro papers and 2) cut 10 papers (all secondary and tough papers for a plethora of classes). All courses (in parentheses below) had a paper, though some (the ones below) had significantly complicated and complex topics I chose to have a 2nd paper on and given that they are all sincerely complex: I decided to shelve them for another year down the road. Thus, LSAT I Pt. II is meant for future times and will include the following topics/papers and perhaps a few or quite a few more. ☐

LSAT I Pt II. – Le Problemes Complexe

TABLE OF CONTENTS

1. The Lawyer Problem (Legal Profession)

2. The Federal Problem (Administrative Law)

3. The Legacy Problem (Trusts & Estates)

4. The Zoning Problem (Educational Law)

5. The 'Reparations Type' Problem (Remedies)

6. The Lack of Resources Problem (Leadership for Women in Law)

7. The Race Problem (Advanced Legal Research)

8. The Federal v. State Problem (Intro to American Legal Systems)

9. The Clients of Big Law Firms Problem (Big Law – The Practice of Large Firms)

10. The Constitution Problem (Constitutional Law)

_____

www.ingramcontent.com/pod-product-compliance
Lightning Source LLC
Chambersburg PA
CBHW052342220526
45465CB00003BA/913